Why Are You So Sad?

Selected Poems of

David W. McFadden

Also by David W. McFadden

Animal Spirits
Anonymity Suite
The Art of Darkness
Canadian Sunset
Country of the Open Heart
Five Star Planet
The Great Canadian Sonnet
Great Lakes Suite
Gypsy Guitar
I Don't Know
An Innocent in Cuba
An Innocent in Ireland
An Innocent in Newfoundland
An Innocent in Scotland
Intense Pleasure
A Knight in Dried Plums
Letters from the Earth to the Earth
A Little Kindness
My Body Was Eaten by Dogs: Selected Poems of David McFadden
A New Romance
On the Road Again
The Ova Yogas
A Pair of Baby Lambs
The Poem Poem
Poems Worth Knowing
The Poet's Progress
The Saladmaker
The Sun Will Not Shine Forever
There'll Be Another
Three Stories and Ten Poems

Why Are You So Sad?

Selected Poems of

David W. McFadden

edited by Stuart Ross

A 4 A.M. BOOK

INSOMNIAC PRESS

Editor for the press: Paul Vermeersch
Selected and edited by Stuart Ross
Introduction copyright © Stuart Ross 2007
Poems copyright © David W. McFadden 2007
All poems in this book are reproduced with the permission of the author.

Library and Archives Canada Cataloguing in Publication

McFadden, David, 1940-   Selected poems / David W. McFadden.

ISBN 978-1-897178-41-6

    I. Title.
PS8525.F32S45 2007   C811'.54   C2007-901105-5

The publisher gratefully acknowledges the support of the Canada Council,
the Ontario Arts Council and the Department of Canadian Heritage
through the Book Publishing Industry Development Program.

Printed and bound in Canada

Insomniac Press
192 Spadina Avenue, Suite 403
Toronto, Ontario, Canada, M5T 2C2
www.insomniacpress.com

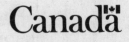

CONTENTS

INTRODUCTION

And a sense of amazement springs up, amazement that we live in a world where the sun continually rises and sets.
— David McFadden, "A Cup of Tea with Issa"

If Frank O'Hara was the poet of "Personism" — recording the minute details of a life lived in New York City among writers and artists — then David W. McFadden might be the poet of "Otherpersonism," recording his fascination with everyone around him: writers, artists, the guy working the convenience store, the woman on the bus, in Toronto, Hamilton, Havana or wherever the poet happens to be.

That's not to say the chameleon-like narrators of David's poems don't play a pivotal role in the works, whether they are McFadden himself, an innocent observer or a plain-spoken killer. But David's poetry, like David, is social. It's interested in people, and in trees, squirrels, dogs and oceans. It's also social in that it wants to be read, and it makes itself readable — not just to academics and to other poets, but to the convenience-store guy and the woman on the bus.

The socialness seems to arise from a deep humanistic impulse in David's work, an interest in and compassion for others that exists contemporaneously with an imbued despair. When David read through the final selection for this volume, he remarked on how *sad* it is. But when I read his work, I feel that he acknowledges sadness — the sadness of mortality, missed opportunity, war — but then revels in a delight and wonder, in even the most ordinary things, and in the privilege of being alive and getting to look at clouds, watch movies, listen to Ella Fitzgerald, walk through a neighbourhood and talk to strangers in bars. Even as a mopey teenage poet, I saw this love-energy in those fantastic McFadden books I stumbled across in the public library. Of course, what also attracted me was how goddamn *funny* these poems so often were.

David was born in Hamilton, Ontario, in 1940, and that's where he grew up. Barely out of his teens, he started up a mimeo poetry mag called *Mountain*, which lasted a respectable four issues. This drew him into contact with some of Canada's finest poets of the era. Then, into his thirties, he was involved in another type of writing altogether: he became a beat reporter for the *Hamilton Spectator*. Perhaps that's where he honed the emphatic clarity of his poetry lines — and his fascination with others.

And just as the (considerably less funny) Austrian poet George Trakl opened his poetry to the mangled bodies he encountered as an army medic during World War I, so McFadden opened his work to the corpses and crimes he reported on during his stint at the Hamilton daily. But there is a magic in David's poetry, which sometimes comes in the form of surrealism and sometimes something closer to magic realism, and it's there whether he's writing about a death at a backyard swimming pool or a chance encounter with a stranger on the main street of Nelson, B.C.

And just as he likely felt a responsibility as a chronicler of facts for the *Spectator*, there's a sense in his poetry that he really has no choice in his role as a poet.

> *... why do things that most people scarcely notice*
> *affect me so, why can't I be like everyone else and simply turn and go*
> *back the way I came without honking? Why do I always have to give a*
> *damn?*
> ("Lion in the Road")

> *You should have cut it off six lines ago*
> *yet it strikes me as poor form for a poet*
> *to refrain from writing while inspired.*

> *Anyone can write when inspired. It takes*
> *a master poet to write while uninspired.*
> *Take me for example. When inspired*
> *I have better things to do than compose.*
> ("Bathing in Diabolic Acid")

The first couple of generations of New York Poets were committed to a poetry that could offer a reader pleasure. So it's no coincidence that McFadden shares so much with O'Hara (who shows up in McFadden's "Frank O'Hara" and "New York," and whose "LANA TURNER HAS COLLAPSED!" is echoed in the "STAN LAUREL CLOSE TO DEATH" line in "Little Spots of Grease"), with the New York School's comedian, Kenneth Koch, and with Ron Padgett, who writes odes to salt shakers and woodpeckers. There are few Canadian poets who offer as much pure pleasure as Dave. In fact, he forbids analysis of his poems.

When I set out to assemble this volume, I envisioned a book that would present, in chronological order, a representative selection of his poems exactly as they were first published. We'd see the trajectory from twenty-something poet to sixty-something poet. David seemed game for such a book, too, and was eager to key in all the poems himself, which he mostly did. He assured me the only changes he'd make were to "correct mistakes" in the originals. "Some of those poems never got an edit!" he told me.

He'd revised many of the poems for *My Body Was Eaten by Dogs*, the 1982 career overview prepared by Dave's old friend George Bowering. And for this volume, he found even more, um, mistakes, ranging from commas and line breaks to a word here and there, the occasional line and sometimes an entire stanza. He really seemed to go after the word "love" in some of those sixties poems.

I asked him whether he wasn't inflicting forty years of experience on works he wrote when he was in his twenties. "They were mistakes," he assured me. "I couldn't let them go by." And the word "love"? Was he getting rid of that because he'd become cynical? "They were mistakes! I used that word way too often."

Truth is, the poems he "corrected" are better now, and reading them through, I didn't feel I was missing anything I experienced with original copies of *Poems Worth Knowing* or *Letters from the Earth to the Earth*. In a few instances, I implored him to go back to the original; sometimes he agreed, sometimes not. He booted out a few poems entirely and suggested replacements. I didn't argue much. David wrote about the urge to revise in the preface to *The Art of Darkness*: "The words are born and die like individual cells of the body and only the form is divine."

And when we were done, I asked him how he'd like to divide the book. Into decades, like Bowering did, or by book? David thought for a bit, and then answered delightedly, "I'll feed the titles into my computer and let it generate a random order! Randomness works well for me." (David wrote some of his greatest poems with the help of coin tosses and the *I Ching*.)

I was disappointed and skeptical, but when he sent me the randomized order the next day and I arranged the poems accordingly, I saw the brilliance of this Zen strategy. This book wouldn't be a narrative tracing the evolution of my favourite Canadian poet's career. It would be a non-hierarchical selection of his life's work to date. That's not to say I don't suspect David — whose mischievous persona is as present as his innocent persona — of tampering with serendipity. Or perhaps I just underestimate serendipity.

A few final notes on this selection. First, I decided to go light on what McFadden calls the Terrafina Trilogy — *Gypsy Guitar*, *There'll Be Another* and *Five Star Planet*. These titles, all published by Talonbooks, are (at least nominally) still in print. With the exception of *Anonymity Suite* (1992) and a few works drawn from above/ground chapbooks, this book favours David's pre-1987 work. Second, there simply wasn't room for many of McFadden's long poems, especially book-length works like "The Poem Poem," "A New Romance" and "The Poet's Progress." Perhaps some enterprising publisher will produce a volume that brings those vital accomplishments together. (There's also nothing here from the weird little chapbook *The Sun Will Not Shine Forever*, which David wrote under the name Wilbur Snowshoe and bill bissett published under his blewointmentpress imprint.)

David told me in an interview for my magazine *Syd & Shirley* in 2005, "From Grade 11 till now I've been writing poems every day, or thinking about it a lot on the occasional day I'd miss. To me an artist had to work every day, it had to be his entire life, or he was a fake. Feel that way even more today."

As I was working on this selection, David sent me a copy of a suite of over 100 sonnets he'd just completed. It was as exciting as anything he'd ever written, and he was pushing into new territory. So, as a look at one poet's career, the book you're holding now is still a work-in-progress. There are intense pleasures here, and intense pleasures to come.

Stuart Ross
Toronto, March 2007

DESIRE BLOSSOMS

You know how you're walking late at night
and the ground's covered with severed human hands
sticking up from the stinking ground like two lips
and the forefinger of each is pointing at you,
swivelling in synch as you slither by,
each badly in need of a manicure? No, the
ground is sprinkled with desire blossoms
sticking up in the air like asparagus stalks,
sometimes spewing dull spurts of blood.
No, the ground is covered with nocturnal robins
each pulling a sleepy earthworm from the earth.
No reason for being alarmed. End of stanza.

Now you're imagining extravagant parking lots
with pairs of red lights going into the ground
below that apartment tower all night long
at the corner of Bay and St. Joseph where a
lady gastroenterologist was stabbed to death
with a screwdriver by a nut with a loose bolt.
It's one of those nights when you say to yourself,
I was wrong, I was too hard-nosed, I didn't
want to take my half of the blame, and any
sense of humour I'd ever had deserted me.
True nobility of spirit lies in crying for the
pain of others and laughing at your own.
My earnest prayer's to die, if I must, laughing.
You could make it yours too, my dearest friend.
Don't be afraid to talk to me. I hear everything you
say even though I have no way of responding and your
busy signal's in synch with my busy heart.
I've never been very fond of surprises
unless it's me who's surprising you.

TRAVELLIN' MAN

My wife asks is it raining out
& I say no
although there are raindrops on the road
& I am all aglow.

How long have I been on the road
as a thought goes through me,
my head dark as a speeding car
with snow tires in rainy summer-night coolness.

It did not rain, the drops dried.
She puts her foot on the rim of the sink
& towels her ankles pink,
puffy white small clouds below the darker —

Something might have come out of the sky & spoken
but I was in the bathroom & couldn't look.

The car sped downhill quite rapidly.
My ears were its wheels.
I was reading a book & couldn't look.
My ears were joined by an axle.

AMERICAN SQUIRREL

The brave little American squirrel sets out on a cold
December day in search of nuts.
He only has eyes for nuts.
And anything that could stop him in his search for nuts.
Such as being run over by a bus.
So you can see that he pays no attention to the cold wind.
Or the blowing leaves dead as ancient carcasses.
Or shoppers shivering in their parkas as
they strive to remember where they parked
their fossilized somnambulistic stinkpots.
But he does pay attention to dogs on the loose,
for a pair of kamikaze dogs a block away
could be soon upon him breathing flames
and fiery sparks through long sharp teeth
and he would never find another nut. But this poem is not
going to be about the kamikaze/terrorist paradox.

Suddenly the savvy squirrel stumbles onto something —
it's even bigger and better than any nut —
it's a giant organic matsu
from some great state or another —
the great state of Washington —
the great state of Hawaii —
completely peeled but with only
one little bite taken out of it.

The squirrel has that apple in its jaws
and he sails up the nearest giant American oak
planted long before the emergence of
our semi-Platonic state-sponsored terrorism
and hides between a pair of slender limbs
so other squirrels cannot see his grins
and try to horn in on his happiness —

and so he eats the whole bloody fruit —
gobbles it down until there is nothing left —
it would be nice to save it for winter but
an apple will go rotten: it's not a nut.

It doesn't occur to him it may be selfish
to be pigging out while others starve
but the stronger he gets
the better for all the squirrels in the world
or so he conveniently philosophizes
in that squirrelly Margaret Thatcher manner.

And the seeds that may ultimately trickle down
someday improbably will sprout up all around
with Hawaiian matsu trees springing up all along
this avenue, providing even better apples
to come for even better squirrels to come.

But let's face it, fellow reader, it takes more
than a chewed-up apple seed to grow a tree —
it takes a plan, and knowledge too, and wisdom.
Never will an edible apple arise from some
stingy squirrel spitting out a seed —
and my sleepy brain cells seem to have agreed....

But take hope, sad-eyed philosophers and seers —
a million brigadiers from right and left hemispheres
have jettisoned their arms and are holding hands
and are singing in my enraptured ears
about their perfect levity, their sweet accord,
and their farewell after all these years
to murder, mayhem, misery, and tears.

NATURE

Nature commits no errors.
— Carl Jung

    I

"Twinkle, Twinkle, Little Star" & "Jingle Bells"
I learned to scratch out on the violin
so I could help my little girl
who is falling behind in music class.

Small child with violin.
I spent the afternoon in the library watching people
spending the afternoon in the library
& caught Ravi Shankar & Yehudi Menuhin on TV.

Small child with violin,
surefooted & full of images as a helicopter.

I spent the evening spending the evening
& spending money in the record shop.

Sat quietly for an hour
then played another song on the little fiddle.

Spent the evening watching TV
& praying for adventure.

Spent three minutes devising
a get-rich-quick scheme.

Dreamt of a beautiful woman
then woke up thinking she was going to kill me.

Set up a wire attached to a shotgun
to shoot trespassers.

Walked down a country road at midnight
praying for flying saucers to come & get me.

II

Nature never makes mistakes, I wrote,
then erased it.
If God had intended elephants to rollerskate
he never would have sunk Atlantis.

A small power can never make an alliance
with a large power
said Nasser
any more than a lamb with a wolf.

Funny the things you remember. Nasser
flying over the pyramids at 30,000 feet
when I was a 15-year-old somnambulist
the year Canadian TV was invented.

Now that I am much older I question
the wisdom of squeezing pimples.
I know that I am the same person essentially
yet an unknown spirit has seized my soul.

When I was 19 I met a man who was to change
my life. We exchanged souls. He died, then
my soul returned to me. But I can't
get rid of his.

When I was 22 I exchanged souls
with a beautiful older woman. When we die

we hope to exchange notes & observations.
Yet I dream she's a monster.

The year I joined the Mafia was the year
the lights went on all over Canada & the year
Ronald Reagan said "Who wouldn't want to hold
the highest office in the world?"

This is a sort of history & history
is a provincial responsibility. We hope to prove
Lee Harvey Oswald knew Joey Smallwood.
When you wish upon a streetlamp.

It was midnight & I looked at the tree
& decided two branches had to be pruned
& when I went out in the morning with my saw
I saw the two branches had fallen off.

I dreamt I sat on a rock at the intersection
of two fateful paths
& all around me the trees were talking.

I dreamt I wrote all night
trying to give what has me by the hair
the opportunity to speak.

I dreamt my work was throwing light
out into the dark night
in out of the sunny day.

III

My daughter will become a famous fiddler
& she will enjoy bandaging my fingers
broken on the day she was born, & I am guilty

of telling her Niagara Falls stopped falling that day
& a snowy owl flew into the house
& died on the kitchen floor
& my Book of Oracles predicted
she'd be born "after the bones are broken."

Also on that day a man from Glace Bay
came to Hamilton & got a job at the Steel Company
& married a girl who could not paint, it made her sick.
"How come all the guys at work, their wives paint
& in this house I have to do all the painting?"
he said & she said "It makes me sick, but don't forget
I do all the gardening. I even mow the lawn
with that heavy monstrous lawnmower."

I won't mention the name of the province
but it starts with a Q & all the people there
are bisexual. Two guys came here from there
& killed a guy from here for $20.
They went back there & spent the $20
printing communist handbills on Albania.

When I went there I arrived there
after leaving here
& knocked on the Prime Minister's door
& he was watching wrestling on TV.
Sit down & watch with me, he said,
I'll go get us a couple of cold ones.
When he came back he said Wrestling? Why
are you watching that crap, that's only for morons.
When I took a sip of beer he said Beer?
You people from Hamilton sure are slobs.

Then he became a beautiful woman
& I began to feel uneasy

then she became a monster with fangs
& I spilled my beer & backed into a corner.

Around the room she flew
cackling "Yes it's true
those two from Q—
were intending to kill YOU!"

IV

Hello, hello, my little friends, I certainly wish you were
a litter of little kittens so I could hear you purr.
A group of 14 Canadian tourists has been found shot to death
by the tomb of the unknown soldier.
We interrupt this newsflash to bring you a bulletin.
The bodies have vanished, & with them the tomb.

Remember when you worked the midnight shift
at the glass factory
& I would walk with you to work
& sleep on the grass outside the plant
& you would wake me up when you finished in the morning —

Remember when I would wake up at night & think of you
& record the time, then you would feel me thinking of you
& record the time, & in the morning we would compare times,
& we were always hours out?

Remember when I phoned you at 2 a.m. & some practical joker
said you had been caught in the glass-crushing machine
& they were pulling pieces of you out of the machine
& I slashed my wrists & in the morning you came out
& found me slumped in the bloody phone booth
& gave me mouth-to-mouth breathing
& bandaged my wrists & saved my life —

And did those feet in ancient time
wade through Canada's endless slime?
Flowers, poems, beautiful music
in this far northern clime?

And we were walking through the vacant shopping centre
at midnight, spring, 1960, full virginal moon,
dizzy in the shopping centre under the moon
that had shone on Troy. Or rather Hamilton
before the shopping centre had been built,
in fact before the racetrack that had been ripped out
to build the shopping centre had been built.
When there were streams bouncing down the escarpment
& seeping through the swamps,
before the beaver dam was ripped out to build
the Pussycat Theatre,

& we held hands & didn't know what was happening
& now we do not know what is happening & hold hands.

        V

Nature was nature before it was born,
just as your mother, cousin, is my aunt.
I do not want to draw attention
to human error.

I have certain tastes
that I will not have exploited
but I refuse to have them distorted
to save them from being exploited.

The mother of us all was never paid
for her idealistic contribution
to the distribution of male & female babies
throughout the countryside.

Throughout the countryside I travelled
tossing my seed to and fro:
this after I ceased
using my mother tongue.

I met a woman who told me
there are certain words I must not utter
speak or write or even think
or I will find myself in another world.

She had her own taboo words, but mine
were not hers, so she told me mine,
but could not tell me hers
because, as do I, she likes this world.

Or at least she liked it then.
I don't know, perhaps
she is gone now, & if I say one of the words
I may find myself with her again, trapped.

I met a woman in her eighties
who nightly dreams of those
who have been dead 50 years,
with clarity.

For there are still those
who like this world.
There are still those
who do not know what is happening.

There are still those
who lust after words
& afterwards they lust
after other things.

There are still those who could not possibly
know what is happening
& they still lust
after what is happening.

VI

If you could see a thought
it would look like a typewriter
& if you could see me now
you would know I am not a thought.

But if you could think of me now
you would know I am a thought
& always will be
every time you think of me.

What about the future?
I asked nature
& nature answered me
flawlessly.

The young friendly trees
flow up from the earth.
They will let you touch them
& listen to them.

There is a rock among the trees
you can sit & listen
& the trees continually say
"Commit no error, commit no error."

"Nothing dies. When you strive
for immortality
you are like a tree striving
to be a tree."

In each piece of air
we draw into our lungs
there is enough power to keep us
alive for a few moments.

It is not my place
to tell you to breathe deeply
for nature commits no errors
& doctors bury their mistakes.

There is enough power
in a glass of water
there is enough power
in 100 bean sprouts

there is enough power
in a motorboat
there is enough power
in the solar system.

Nowhere is there not enough
power, at least nowhere
I have seen, unless
I have buried a mistake.

It is not my place
to talk about power,
I am only the man
who cuts the grass.

Perhaps I have been wrong
to talk of power
perhaps it would have been more proper
to continue with air.

Perhaps it would have been wrong
to continue with air
for I am only a man
who knows nothing about air power.

But then again I have not
criticized
any member of the armed forces
for discussing air power

& of course no one
has criticized me,
but I am fearful
of being in error

for to be in error
is to be out of nature
looking in, there is
pain in that.

For pain reminds us
an error has been made
& is then a part
of an error.

For pain reminds us
no error has been made
& a lie reminds us
no error can ever be made.

To err is superhuman.
To forgive is to
commit an error,
unnatural, divine.

Is it natural to be perfect?
Is it perfectly natural
to cut the grass
with a power mower?

I do not know everything.
Nor do I know
exactly what I do know
so I will write some more.

I will repeat this line:
I do not know everything
& I will repeat it again:
I do not know everything

& I could repeat it forever
not knowing if it be true
for I do not know
what I mean by I.

Nature nature on the wall
Nature nature in the hall
Nature grabs me by the hair
I am nature's living doll.

Wherever error flies
it hits its mark.
Nothing dies,
the night is dark.

AFTER LULLABY

Sleep, sweet baby-blossom, like the
grass and vines. Hair growing,
fingernails growing, moon-
cells
     of bone and muscle
                 groaning
moaning sighing dividing dying.
Sleep and grow, sly bamboo-baby.

Sleep all night and when the sun
comes in the window I'll come &
get you
     and our brains will be
all bright again and we will have
breakfast and
study the eggs.

PIGEONS

I toss a handful of popcorn on the grass
& suddenly the park is full of pigeons.
Strings of light left over from Christmas
dangle down from small maples.
A small fat boy walks by
& the pigeons fly away.
The boy picks up a piece of popcorn
& puts it in his mouth
& flies away.

THREE ON A TREE

Why am I writing
Imaginary haiku?
    Because they're not there.

        *

    High school wrestling team
Gets fired up when the coach bites
    Heads off live sparrows.

        *

        Excuse me, darling.
    I'm trying to write haiku.
        What season is this?

        *

Why do we worry?
We're merely leaves on a tree.
    Let the tree worry.

NUMBER

Seven cities I visited
In seven days and in each city
I was chased down seven streets
By seven dogs. At the age of seven
I had seven friends and seven enemies
And saw *Seven Brides for Seven Brothers*
Seven times. Seven blind hemophiliacs
Engaged me to give them seven lessons
In the seven deadly games of chance.

Humphrey Bogart and Lauren Bacall
Appeared together in four films.
My first memory: four windmills
With four blades each, slowly revolving.
Sandra Rabinovitch is four months' pregnant.
There are four *fleurs-de-lis* in the flag of Quebec
And four stars known as the Trapezium
At the core of the Orion Nebula.

Master Sekito, seven feet seven,
Was born in A.D. 777.
Mother had seven ways of regarding you,
One for each child she bore.

À la Recherche du temps perdu
Has seven parts. There are seven stars
In the Pleiades. The Hamilton painter
J. E. H. Macdonald made
Seven trips to the Rocky Mountains,
One each August from 1924
To 1930. Father's seventy-seven:
With teeth, eyes, taste and everything.

Mira, a red giant in Cetus,
Is two hundred light-years from Myra Segal,
Who says her life hasn't been the same
Since she focussed a scope on the Moons of Jupiter.
Mira flares up to shine more brightly
Than Polaris then fades away to nothing
In an irregular cycle of eleven months.
It's the only star known to be non-spherical,
Like a partially deflated beach ball.

I smoked seven cigars in seven hours
And caught seven fish in seven rivers.
Mother bore me in the seventh month.
I ate seven ice cream cones in a row
And failed grade seven seven times.
I found seven skeletons in seven closets,
Seven dead cats in seven backyards
And I wrote this poem at forty-nine.

MORNING MOON

The face of a dying child
amid dawn's exploding rays.

MY BROTHER'S POETRY

Glenn Gould dropped in and started playing Bach's Two and Three Part
Inventions on the little Yamaha which by chance I'd just had tuned.
And my father wouldn't listen, he kept telling me stories about being
on a ship in the Arctic Ocean during the war. He was telling me how
certain things came to be and he told me all about the war and how it
started. I kept confusing oceans and deserts. He said the ocean is like the
lake only bigger and the desert is like the beach only bigger. Then I was
on my father's ship, standing at his side, Bach still in the air, as the ship
passed through a narrow channel between two mountains of ice. It was
scary as being born. I told my father how brave he was. "I'm not brave,
son," he said, gravely, "in fact I'm seriously considering killing myself,
and by God I am going to kill myself." With that he jumped off the ship
and landed on top of one of the mountains of ice. "Wait for me, Dad," I
shouted, and soon I was on top of the mountain with him. It wasn't all that
cold. We slid down the other side like a pair of penguins. At the bottom
there were some little houses. It looked like Hiroshima on the final morning.
Babies were being born, men and women making love, parachutes appeared
to be falling slowly. Picasso came up to me, did a happy little dance,
and slapped me on the back. William Blake went into the outhouse and
slammed the door. I remember I'd been arguing with Glenn Gould about
who was the greater artist, Blake or Picasso. He chose Blake and I Picasso.

I wandered through the narrow streets and found the farmhouse where my
Uncle Cecil and Aunt Clara used to live. This was the hill I tried to climb
when I was a kid. It wasn't a mountain of ice then. It wasn't dangerous.
It was sunny and there was a bluebird on every fencepost. You could hear
a cow moo three miles away. All this really happened long ago, and it
somehow explains everything: now I know why I am the way I am and why
you are the way you are. You are with me. We're all climbing down ladders.
My brother is acting smart. He too threatens to kill himself, then falls
accidentally off his ladder and down the mountain of ice. He falls slowly
like a parachute bomb. You try to save him by pulling on the rope
but as you pull it his head falls off. You become almost hysterical. My

father appears and puts his coat over my brother's body. He picks up the head and puts it under the blanket too. He is serene. "I was expecting something like this," he says, oddly untroubled. "He'd been acting so strangely lately. He wasn't always like this." My father pulls out an old book of poems authored by my brother. They are beautiful poems, with long exquisite lines that branch out and seem to reach up to heaven. No poems like them. Nice edition too. I had no idea my brother could write such poetry and suddenly I'm crying. And there's a blinding explosion of light.

ECKANKAR

The President of the United States was visiting Canada. He made a speech in the House of Commons. Then the Prime Minister of Canada made a speech. I listened to it all on the radio. Then I switched over to a station from Spokane. During the U.S. newscast, they didn't mention the President at all, never mind that he was in Canada.

I went for a walk along Baker Street. The parking meters had all been removed, leaving only the stands, upright tubes along the curb every ten feet. It was an experiment to increase business.

A car with U.S. plates pulled up at the curb. The driver got out, a fat guy with a cigar and Bermuda shorts. Gee, I thought, here he is visiting Canada just like the President of the United States. I wonder if he's listening to the speeches on the CBC. I wonder what he thinks of the coverage.

The driver stood next to one of the decapitated parking meters. He fished in his pocket and pulled out some change. Isn't that funny, I thought, he doesn't notice the parking meter's been removed.

Then a strange thing happened. The U.S. tourist dropped a coin down the inside of the parking meter stand.

I looked up and noticed a second-floor window with "Eckankar" painted on it. Through the window I could see, on the wall, a huge photo of that guy, the Eckankar guru.

Just then somebody whipped open the window and threw something out. It was money. All kinds of paper money floating through the air. The U.S. tourist and I were the only ones around. The money floated to the sidewalk. We picked it all up and stuffed it in our pockets.

Then the U.S. tourist gave me a strange look and got in his car and drove away.

I went straight home and counted the money. I had almost $2,000.

Boy, that Eckankar is some religion!

LITTLE SPOTS OF GREASE

When I first saw you
you were sitting in the front of a King Street bus
& as I watched
you pulled a kitten from a paper bag in your lap
& began stroking & tickling it
with unselfconscious childish glee.

That was around 1952.
You were perhaps 30
but it was hard to tell with your round flat face,
your shapeless body, thick rimless glasses,
red hair & baggy clothing.

You paid no attention to others on the bus
& the others paid no attention to you
& I began to think you were some weird vision
created specially for my fascination.

Since then I have seen you many times
always on the move,
cutting along King Street
always as if you had someplace to go,
some important destiny to meet
but I always secretly knew
your destiny involved
nothing but visions of funny kittens
& dreams of hairy sword-waving angels.

One night last week I was sipping coffee
in Towers Restaurant on King Street just west of Mary
& there you were sitting in a booth
not eating anything as far as I could see
but just sitting there immersed in dreams

your eyes focussed on the damp nose
of some imaginary newborn kitten,
your red hair drawn into a bun
& your face not aged a year in 20
but of a peculiarly high ruddiness
as if you had developed high blood pressure.

You got up & walked to the cash register
to buy a Coffee Crisp chocolate bar
& it was obvious you had gained a lot of weight
& your long grey skirt & grey cardigan
were stained with little spots of grease
& your green running shoes
were torn & dirty.

As you turned you bumped
into a leather-jacketed motorcycle kid
then shortsightedly looked up into his face
as if you innocently & curiously
wanted to know what he looked like.

Soon you were back in your booth of dreams
chewing on your chocolate bar so sweetly
& I felt sad because in 20 years
you've never once looked into *my* face
with innocent curiosity.

And last night you were in Al's Smoke Shop
thumbing through dirty tabloids imported from the U.S.A.
& I was with a loudmouth friend who was trying
to find thick magazines to use in his plan
for smuggling razorblades into Yugoslavia
& your face came out from behind a tabloid,
on the cover was a full-page photo of Stan Laurel
sitting in a wheelchair in a dirty dressing gown

in a creepy nursing home in Southern California
with a headline screaming STAN LAUREL CLOSE TO DEATH,
& you quizzically looked up into the face of my friend
& avoided looking into my sensitive eyes as usual.

When I left the store I knew
I will die & you will die
but you will never know
you had a gentle friend in me.

EIGHT INCHES OF SNOW

I

Should I let Alison take Natalie to school
when it's bring-your-pet-to-school day?
Should I allow myself the pleasure of writing poems
when the idea of being a poet sickens me?
Should I get mad when the kids throw food at each other?
Should I let Herman take over the court beat?
Should I wash the dishes while Joan takes a nap?
Should I? Should I? Should I?

II

Children, eat your supper.
Quit pulling each other's hair.
Quit sitting on the same chair.
Quit hugging and kissing.
Quit living.

III

When I was an industrious adolescent
I wanted to be a beautiful poet.
When I got older my ambition modified —
I wanted to be a beautiful person.
Now I'm middle-aged I want to be
an alligator.
I want to bite myself and everybody.
Should I? Should I? Should I?

IV

Do it, Daddy. Do it, Daddy. Do it.
An awesome concavity has enveloped Spain.
Jennifer put her hand palm down on the table
then Alison put her hand palm down on Jennifer's
then Jennifer put her other hand palm down on Alison's
then I put my hand down on both of theirs.
Then we all broke out laughing.

V

Eight inches of snow fell on Southern Italy
the day after Pierre Trudeau got married.
Four reindeer at the North Pole were picked up
by helicopter and deposited at the
South Pole. I wanted to be pure.
I didn't want to be hypocritical.
I wanted to have one side only.
This is Bruce Marsh speaking
for Kraft Foods in Canada.

VI

Although it was midnight the sky was bright.
The white snow stretched out to the horizon.
A dot appeared on the horizon
and got closer and closer.
As the dot approached I could see
it was more of a pin-prick than a dot.
It came right up to me and looked as if
it were about to speak. I
reached out my hand and erased it.

VII

I preach forgiveness, forgetfulness
and historical research.
I preach in one ear and out the other
faster than a speeding bullet.
A new-hatched chick hops out of the sky
at every crack of thunder.
Everyone should wear a blue T-shirt
with a left breast pocket.
Quit smoking and live longer.

VIII

I wonder what happened to Harry Howard.
He was that clean-cut baby-faced Calvinist
contrabassoon player I knew 15 years ago.
He only had one navel but it was novel.
There is a time and place for being sentimental.
Ech! My tongue is in my mouth!
Little stars dance in my backyard.
(Line erased here) (something about square dancing)
Yesterday I saw a six-month-old Irish terrier.

ON THE ROAD AGAIN

It's all part of growing up.
I know Canada is the only country in the world more American than the
U.S.A.
We're so stupid we accept Colonel Sanders and reject Frank O'Hara.
But I was sitting at the bar in a pub in Carleton Place, Ontario, at 6 p.m. on
Tuesday, April 6, 1976, just before the Stompin' Tom Connors concert
in Smiths Falls.
The guys were talking about their snowmobiles.
Suddenly it happened.
In spite of the ugliness of so much of our history, our culture and our lives,
ugliness that will probably never end, I felt at home.
My heart, normally the size of a dried plum, grew to fill the room, the
town, the province, the whole damned country.
And these lines came bubbling up.
If I'm ever remembered, this is what I'd like to be remembered by:

> *Toss*
> *a dart at the map of Canada,*
> *where it lands is*
> *where you'll find me.*

COUNTRY HOTEL IN THE NIAGARA PENINSULA

The guy was shooting pool. I stopped to watch.
He missed an easy shot and the cue ball
hopped the cushion and crashed to the floor.
"I'm bad luck," I murmured apologetically
as I scurried to the door. "You sure are,"
the guy yelled after me, his voice melting
into the evening fog, streaked with light from the
streetlamps and the headlights of cars on Highway 8.

Everybody understands my poetry. There is nothing
hidden. A large mind examines a small mind,
mounts it like a butterfly, splits it open
under intense light, an ongoing autopsy
in the morgue of all our lives.
You know everything you need to know.

DEATH OF A MAN WHO OWNED A SWIMMING POOL

In my bathing suit & sunglasses
carrying a portable radio
& a large bottle of Quick Tan
I walked into this guy's backyard
on Mountain Brow Boulevard
He'd never seen me before
He was sitting on a lawn chair
with a gin & tonic
as I put down my stuff without a word
walked out on his diving board
bounced up and down a few times
& plunged in

swam around for about 10 minutes
climbed out
dried myself off
turned on my radio
put on some Quick Tan

The guy just sat there looking at me
Oh hi I said as if I'd just noticed him
I hope you don't mind me using your swimming pool
I haven't got one myself
Sure a hot summer we're having eh?

The guy didn't say a thing
He had a red face
& it was getting redder
& it wasn't sunburn

I think I'll have one more swim before I go
I said & plunged in again

When I climbed back out a few minutes later
the guy had fallen out of his chair
& was lying on his face on the patio

I turned him over
He was dead

THE SPILL

In a century-old vandalized cemetery
overlooking the blue Saugeen
I inspect my bicycle for damage
after falling in soft sand.

Below, tiny fishermen in hip boots
angle at midstream.

Steep narrow mud paths drop
from here to there.

On the far side of the river
in huge smooth green velvet fields
farmers cut hay.

WHEN I AM DEAD

After "Afterwards" by Thomas Hardy (1840-1928)

If in the dusk with the quietness of an eyelid's blink
A hawk soars through the shadows to alight
Upon the ancient wind-warped upland thorn,
Will some dear old friend stop and think
Of me in my recent return to my eternal home
And say: "To him this must have been a familiar sight"?

And when my bell of quittance rolls through the gloom
As a hedgehog scurries over the moonswept lawn
And a crossing breeze muffles the bell like a yawn
For but a moment, till the bell renews its boom,
Will they say I'd have noticed such an auditory feature
And that I'd have wanted to save this innocent creature?

When I am dead and Time's hunting horn
Blasts away as it did before I was born,
Will a child pick up a piece of doggish excrement
And with puppy-like innocence wolf it down
And will someone, perhaps a passing bureaucrat,
Say: "Mr. Hardy would have noticed that"?

When folks hear that my body has been stilled at last,
Will those who will see my face no more
Stand late at night quietly by the snow-filled door
Looking up and watching the stars stream past?
And while picking their nose and scratching their fleas
Remember that I had an eye for such mysteries?

When Time has evicted me and latched its gate
And the month of May causes everyone to copulate
Under the trees with their leaves flapping like wings

Throwing to the breeze their smelly underthings
Will one of my neighbours pause, suddenly clairvoyant,
And say: "Mr. Hardy would have loved to join in"?

BEVERLY REPORT

Driving through Beverly Township
tiny villages like Valens
mud roads strangely marked
roads at a lower level
than the surrounding swamp
and the heavy summer rains
have raised the swamp level
till it's almost a lake —
old reality of Beverly Swamp
where in the early fifties
I learned to use snowshoes
and in the late fifties
other things.

Driving through
like a cork in the river
wanting to be the whole river
at once and forever
brief visions of beautiful people
throwing dead rabbits into the car
or walking with friends at roadside
and so little can I know
of what is most familiar
I want to become God
and so do, breaking
riddles of time and space
and find it a Big Nothing
& re-enter my human form
full of renewed respect
for my ignorance.

MARGARET HOLLINGSWORTH'S TYPEWRITER

I was eating scrambled eggs in the Shamrock Restaurant
and the eggs tasted like Chinese food
so I said to the waitress I'm a person
who likes Chinese food but doesn't like
my eggs in the morning to taste like chicken fried rice
and she laughed and said it must have been
the green onions and suggested the next time
I come into the Shamrock for breakfast
I specify that I want Canadian green onions
with my scrambled eggs or I'll get Chinese again

and I said there won't be another time,
this is it, I'm a widely respected blah blah and blah
and well-regarded in the community too
and shouldn't have to subject myself
to such bad food. I'm finished, I said.
This used to be my favourite Irish-Chinese restaurant
in the entire West Kootenay
but this is it, I'm never coming back —
and through the kitchen door I could see
the Chinese chef covering his ears with his hands.

And so I went to pay my bill
and this is the really embarrassing part,
this is why I'm writing this poem
by hand, pencil on paper, because Margaret Hollingsworth's
typewriter has a three-prong plug
and all the outlets in the house are two-prongers
and her adapter is up at the college
and I begged her to let me cut the third prong off
so I could use her typewriter
because I had a simply overwhelming
desire to write this poem and she refused
and I told ... oh, never mind all that.

This is the embarrassing part. After complaining
so vociferously about the eggs I went to pay my bill
and discovered I had no money with me
so I had to go home and get my wallet
and bring it back to the restaurant
making myself a liar for having said
this is it, I'm never coming back.
The waitress was very nice about it all.

Is it hard to write poetry?
Yes, I would say it is. For instance
in this poem I didn't know whether to start
by talking about the scrambled eggs
or the Smith Corona. And I didn't have
a lot of time to think about it
because I simply had to start the poem,
it was that urgent,
and then you have to torture yourself
wondering if it's all right to write about
writing in a poem and you keep resolving
never again to write about writing
and you always break your resolve.
It's as if writing has a will of its own
and wants to be written about
just like Margaret Hollingsworth's
typewriter.

BASEBALL LONELINESS

Baseballs as multitudinous
As raindrops pelt a log cabin
In the middle of a meadow
As mellifluous as a dream.
A deluge of flying baseballs
Increasing in intensity.
The cabin seems about to implode.

My meditations have been spoiled.
I venture out to order the players
To sit down and try to enjoy
The silence of the golden moment
But as soon as the screen door slams shut
The baseball bombardment comes to a halt.
No one as far as the eye can see.
A rainbow quivers over the hill.

Silently I examine one of the balls.
    It turns out to be a shiny apple.
        I take a bite. Delicious looking
            But terribly sour and full of worms.
                There's a set of bleachers at the edge of the woods.
        Kirby Puckett and Rickey Henderson
    Are sitting there laughing at me as I
Fall to my hands and knees and vomit.

My friends and I when we were kids
Would take up collections and draw straws
To see who would get to go to the movies.
And when the winner returned he'd tell
The others the plot in great detail:
We were terrible kids who did terrible things
To smaller kids and animals.

Organized sport was anathema.
We lied about everything, stole from stores,
Smeared butter on our hair and smoked speed.
We formed little bands of nasty anarchists
Who remembered dialogue from all the movies.
We were too cowardly to take baseball,
Hockey, football, lacrosse seriously.
Those other guys, the ones we hated,
Serious about sports, they never lied.

LENNOX ISLAND

They're more beautiful than the angels of heaven
the beautiful Micmac children of Lennox Island
as all through the long summer they dive, dive, dive
off the dock into the warm tidal waters of Malpeque Bay.
Sometimes they join hands and leap in en masse
then resurface with a gasp, dark hair streaming
and dark eyes flashing in the sun.
From early morning to early evening they dive,
careful to avoid the poisonous jellyfish
which they sometimes call bloodsuckers
and pick like giant mushrooms and flip onto the dock
to die, to fry in the hot sun like eggs,
the dock coated with fading remains
of the summer's harvest and stains
of previous summers.

        It's hard to believe
there are children elsewhere more beautiful
than the beautiful Micmac children of Lennox Island,
aristocratic, oriental, magical and shining with joy.
As for me, the water is too full of bloodsuckers
and the current too strong for me to swim
and I remain silent, strained, and wish I could vanish
for fear they'll flee or become somehow tainted
by my clumsy poisonous presence
and so I strive to become relatively pure
and I invite life to flow through my body
as it flows through the bodies of these children
but I simply become more and more aware
of my powers of destruction and I quietly leave.

And I believe these children are my ancestors
and I believe these children populated the once-sacred earth
and I believe Lennox Island and across the bay
Bird Island, Hog Island, and maybe even part of the
Prince Edward Island mainland
is the birthplace of the human race
and I believe that since that glorious day
we've become more and more stupid in every way.

But I'm not about to immolate myself
because of the imminent death of an ancient race
and I'm thankful fate has given me a glimpse
of all this beauty before it's gone forever.
And on a hill overlooking the dock where the children play
is a curiously twisted hunk of metal.
It is a World War I cannon
that appears to have suffered a direct hit
and there is a plaque to the memory
of the nine Lennox Island men
who were killed in that horrible white-man's war
that war that failed to destroy
that widely held belief in Caucasian superiority
except in the minds of non-Caucasians

and standing quietly watching me
as I try to swallow my foolish tears
is a tall young man of pure African descent
who tells me he's a student from Calgary
who volunteered to spend the summer working
with the 200 Micmac residents of Lennox Island
and he tells me the Micmacs of Lennox Island
are a shy people who desire as little contact as possible
with the white occupants of Prince Edward Island
but they're an industrious group of people
who are perhaps the world's best oyster farmers

and he predicted the beautiful children on the dock
would eventually leave Lennox Island
for Summerside, Charlottetown,
or maybe even Halifax or Moncton,
but they would return after a short time
disillusioned, sick in spirit
and spend the rest of their lives on Lennox Island.

THE SLIPPERY WIG

I sat next to her on the bus
She kept adjusting her short-cut black wig
It must have been a cheap one
It kept slipping

I have an appointment with my lawyer at two
she said & I thought I'd just ride around
the bus line till then.
All the people, it's better than TV
& no commercials.

I've got seven kids, & separated from my husband
two years.
My oldest boy is in the retarded school in London.
The Children's Aid wants to take my second boy
but I don't want them to.
I'm going to get a lawyer to fight it.
I'm used to having the boy around the house.
I would miss him.

THIS POEM HAS A GOOD TITLE

I was thinking of you
& wrote a handful of poems.

I'm a poem specialist!

More poems to write than tears in the ocean
sad to think I'll never get most of them written
especially the good ones.

Maybe I should just specialize in good poems
No, I could never stoop that low
I want to work among the humble poems
poems that can't afford the high cost of justice
the have-not poems that don't know where to turn.

But there's so many of them!
Who's next?
Geez, it's hopeless.

Maybe I should just specialize in titles.
Instead of writing 10,000 poems this lifetime
I should write 10,000,000 titles.

I'm sure people would understand
& would be strangely grateful

& if all the poets would give up writing their daily poem
& started turning out something like 100 titles a day
— if there's a million poets in all languages
that'd be 36-1/2 trillion titles every year —

Maybe something glorious would happen to the world.

MY CRIMINAL RECORD

Fined $50 for ejaculating on the step of the Planned Parenthood Clinic

Fined $10 for trying to stuff a $20 bill into a coffee machine

Fined $2 for molesting a policewoman

Three months in jail for accidentally touching a hitchhiker on the knee while shifting gears

Fined $200 for lending my pen to an ambulance attendant

Suspended sentence for cutting my daughter's fingernails in a public park

Six months probation for chewing gum in a fire hall

Fined $49.95 for sniffing the base of a fire hydrant

A week on the psychiatric ward for signing a false name in a funeral home guest book

Sternly reprimanded for crying in a laundromat

MANDALA DREAM

There was a cop at the intersection
directing traffic
but there was
no traffic
& no people

with the cop's cruiser
parked at the roadside
and I came by —
hopped in the cruiser,
drove away.

Driving away
furiously
towards an exploding
horizon.

POEM FOR JENNIFER TO READ MANY YEARS FROM NOW

November 7, 1969

I

No way to know if you'll remember anything of this year
but I want you to know how much fun it was
& as I write this you're sitting next to me on the chesterfield
little thigh to big thigh your fingers getting in the way
as you laughingly try to pick my words of blue ink off the white page
as soon as they are made.

This morning I was on the phone & Joan had to go to the store
& you stood there crying, your pink bear in your arm, your doll
& a big snot hanging out your right nostril,
cried so loud I couldn't hear the Hydro employee I was talking to
& had to excuse myself to go to you.

& I was at the table eating Shredded Wheat
& you were in your high chair eating Puffed Rice
& I looked out the corner of my eye at you
& you lowered your eyes with a little smile,
slowly lowered your face almost into the Puffed Rice
                    — your very own blush!

People say I'm going to be so hurt cause all little girls
grow up to be absolute bitches
but Daddy Daddy Daddy Daddy Daddy Daddy
you chant over & over as you zip & unzip the pillowslip zipper
& smash me across the face with the pillow,
lean on my head & grab my pen.

Baby Jennifer a living thing, a human that has to die
& go through all kinds of agony,

the female agony that is so different from the male
& yet is so the same —
                        the pure physical cycle of terror
maybe starvation, imprisonment, bullets, bombs, liquid fire
there is so little your father can protect you from
& the pain of the search for a way of life among the terrors
the non-physical pains & the pain of growing & trying to gain control
& the pains that fall away as little discoveries fall into place
& in your case what will those discoveries lead to?
& although I may not be able to see the form that emerges
I know now the form will come & whatever it is
I'll be amazed & joyful or actually am at the moment
as I know it will come.
                        Something very small.

A tiny perfection among tiny perfections
& a passionate absorption
                        in the Jenniferness of the world.

      II

Everything you do kills me this year
even those rotten baby things like dropping a turd on the floor
or getting hold of the lipstick & smearing it everywhere
climbing up on top of the fridge & knocking the radio off (it still plays!)
eating safety pins, cigar butts,
biting the cat.

I wonder what you'll think about when you read these poems I write,
not that I care, poems aren't important,
but it would be nice to know what you'll think of me
say when you're 20 & I'm in my forties.
Doesn't matter to me what you think of me
but I really think I'm going to like you a lot,
not just because you're a cute baby or anything like that

but there's something about you, I worry about a lot of kids I see
but I know with you that you can't turn out wrong no matter what.
Out of all the adults I know there are lots I like a lot, even love
but only about 3 or maybe 4 who really please me & never fail to do so
3 or 4 I can just sit back & watch forever they are so perfect,
& I know you're going to be one of them.
Nothing can happen to change that
except maybe some horrible violent accident
whether personal or on a large scale.

    III

We had fun
           & I learned a lot from you in 1969
We laughed a lot
             & you broke my heart like an acorn

Grow grow grow little child, grow inside your shape
you're going to be a great teacher in everything you do.
I'll be me & you'll be you
& if you need me snap your fingers
& the things you've taught me already, shown me in yourself
I'll be seeing them everywhere.

THE ROCKIES

When we walk to the horizon
we are amazed to find things
as small as they seemed
— Robert Fones

No wonder the gods are so aloof
and also politicians who fly a lot
said I with sorrow
as I sat sipping Air Canada reserve
German wine
and listening to the mighty Ninth Symphony
30,000 feet above the Rockies.

Perhaps a party of ant-like climbers
is stranded on one of those puny
ice-capped peaks far below
the wind howling, food gone, no hope
but to sink into eternal sleep.

I'm going to stop looking out the window
this gives the wrong perspective on things
I thought then started looking down again —
God, if Hitler could have seen these views
he probably would have killed more Jews.

The stewardess stops and I ask her
for help with the crossword puzzle
and compliment her on the wonderful
stereo selections, and I suggest
Air Canada black out the windows
for this kind of looking down on the world
is okay for great novelists like Tolstoy or Hardy
but what can it do for ordinary folk like me

but bring out our latent cruelty
and she laughs and walks away

and what if that flimsy wing suddenly
snapped under the awful pressure I presume
is out there?
            Would I remain calm
as the plane plummeted down?

Of course you would, immortal bard,
murmurs my agreeable frontal lobe
while somewhere at the back of my brain
a woman's voice, the voice of the future, whispers
You'd fall to pieces long before you hit the ground
and I for one would be glad to see that happen.

A MOMENT IN THE LIFE OF THE MEMBERS OF THE
GRADUATING CLASS OF ARNPRIOR HIGH SCHOOL, 1976

It was the day after Northrop Frye
appeared on prime-time TV and called
the poets the mapmakers of the national imagination

and one poor fellow raised his hand
and said "Mat? But people walk all over
mats, don't they?"

And I had to laugh and say *map*,
not *mat*, and all the others laughed
and even he laughed

and later a kid stood up
and said "How do you get your
inspiration? For instance …
do *we* inspire you?"

and through the window you could see
the Ottawa River, the April river-ice
breaking up and flowing downstream.

LION IN THE ROAD

It was lying in the intersection of Bloor and Avenue Road, a giant
lion larger than six elephants, each tooth the size of a fire hydrant
but sharper. It was having a snooze, it took up the entire intersection
and its tail stretched out lazily all the way down to Bedford Road. Its eyes
were open but not seeing much, not noticing the incredible traffic jam,
incredible because no one was honking, incredibly quiet traffic jam: cars
were making cautious U-turns and heading quietly back the way they came.
Basically though it was business as usual. Fashionable ladies in chic
clothing stores weren't coming out to stare, they just kept trying on
the latest fashionable dresses. People in chic restaurants continued
eating lunch, nothing about giant lions in the newspaper, so why look?
A Toronto newspaper columnist and a famous novelist from Connecticut
came out of Bemelman's where they'd been drinking white housewine,
came out without paying and walked by the lion without even a glance.
It was as if the lion had been lying there since the days of the Family
Compact. Or at least since Hugh Garner got banned from the Press Club.
There was the sense that the lion hadn't been officially approved for
notice. Toronto's like that, the sort of city where the day after the famous
travel writer came out with a story complaining that people in Toronto
never talk to strangers everyone started talking to strangers. Someone
I didn't know actually spoke to me in an elevator. And I answered! But
back to the lion. Even tourists and conventioneers with Hi-My-Name-Is
stickers on their lapels merely glanced at the lion before turning away
to point out to each other noteworthy examples of Victorian architecture.
Nobody seemed nervous, surprised, concerned, nobody seemed to be rushing
off to phone the cops or the zoo, though it's obvious this lion didn't escape
from any zoo, no zoo in the world could handle lions this size. Fortunately,
it didn't seem to be hungry, though I wondered what it had been eating,
a lion that size could eat sixteen dogs a day easy and I didn't see any dogs.

So I sat on a bench in front of the Royal Ontario Museum and wondered
what it was about me, why do things that most people scarcely notice
affect me so, why can't I be like everyone else and simply turn and go

— 70 —

back the way I came without honking? Why do I always have to give a damn? And as I watched, the lion stiffened, began ascending into the sky, became smaller and smaller and floated away behind a mass of cloud in the shape of a lion. In no time traffic was back to normal. Honk!

FOR DWIGHT EISENHOWER ON HIS DEATH

March 28, 1969

"We can't let those Communists take over in Viet Nam,"
he said after the French were yanked.
"What would we do for tin & tungsten?" (what the hell's tungsten?)
"We must set up a Pro-American Puppet Government
in Sigh-Gone." It made so much sense
& he was so honest.

        He'd outlived his world
& didn't know it. He stepped out of
Gasoline Alley, Kansas, & it died behind him.
Gasoline Alley'd been cancelled by the Toronto *Globe & Mail*
a few months before his death — what would he have thought?

A naked Viet Conger with a bomb strapped to his back
ran into an American compound & exploded
killing no one but himself, unknown, unnamed,
& the next day Eisenhower was dead.

THE DEATH OF GREG CURNOE

What a painting that would make
THE DEATH OF GREG CURNOE
huge epic panorama
the size of an airport billboard
the size of a Dorval mural
larger than those billboards along the
Melacón in Havana Cuba saying
Sí por Cuba
(often translated as Sigh for Cuba)
or *Esta Tierra Es 100% Cubano*
(even Fidel admits that's a whopper)
large enough in other words to say
without embarrassment here is a death
worth considering worth paying attention to
here is a death to ponder deeply the drastic
end of a life to be inspired by forever

I knew Greg Curnoe
he was a friend of mine
he was my best friend but many
felt he was their best friend
everybody who knew Greg thinks of himself
as having been Greg's best friend
(which is the way it should be)
Greg was like that
he cared for me everyone knew that
when I was suicidal in seventy-nine
(and semi-suicidal in seventy-seven)
he went way out of his way to help me
and now he's gone
I must have had a premonition
because a month before he died
I spent an afternoon in his studio

embarrassing him by telling him
how much I loved him
how great a human being he was
how magnificent an artist he was
how much I valued our friendship

Who could ever have imagined a poem
or a painting with the title
THE DEATH OF GREG CURNOE
who could ever have imagined Greg dead
butterflies or belugas going extinct
but Greg dead never
Greg would outlive everybody he'd still
be cycling and painting
well into the twenty-first century
and then at a highly advanced age
with his work behind him
with all his best friends dead
even his grandchildren all grown up
his heart would quietly stop pumping as he
watched Bugs Bunny on TV and saying
Hey Sheila come and look at this
Geez Sheila this is really good

I would do the painting myself
it would be large of course
of heroic dimensions
I would paint it in the Jack Chambers style
like Chambers' view of the Macdonald-Cartier Freeway
Even though Greg Curnoe died in early November
I would paint it while listening to Holly Cole singing
I'll be seeing you in every lovely summer's day

You would see the thirteen cyclists
arranged in two ranks
entering stage left across the canvas
riding along a quiet peaceful Southern Ontario
tree-lined two-lane highway
a few yellow leaves on the trees
maple leaves of course because they're maple trees
and it's symbolic of Greg's love of his country

In the distance far off the side of the road
a barn floats in a lake of early November floodwater
it really isn't floating it's an optical illusion
all the cyclists are looking at it they are looking
off to the side as they ride over this little bridge

Then in the upper left-hand corner where the road
crests a little hill
you see a pickup truck and the driver is also
looking off to the left at the magic floating barn
both to the left and the right of the road
the fields are flooded with water

The driver is transfixed he's been driving
all the way down from Barrie
it's ten in the morning
there is a chill in the air
the sky is full of death
Greg has been at the front of the rank
it is his turn to go to the back
he is falling back
the cyclists at the front are bracing
for a steep hill coming up
the sky is full of death
a few angels have covered their eyes with their wings

The sky fades away into infinity
floating here and there in the sky dimly
are some of Greg Curnoe's most famous paintings

But if I painted the painting myself
it would be a terrible mess I can't even draw
we couldn't get Jack Chambers to do it because
although Jack Chambers was Greg Curnoe's best friend
Jack Chambers has been dead since 1978 and besides
what painter would paint a painting from someone else's mind

Maybe we could get John B. Boyle to paint it
because John B. Boyle was also Greg's best friend
he would be even better than Jack Chambers
because Chambers is dead Boyle is alive
he wouldn't mind painting a painting out of
somebody else's mind especially since
it's probably in his mind too it's in all our minds
although it might not have occurred to him yet
and he could paint it in the Chambers style or even
in his own style if he thought it more appropriate

I'm walking around El Museo Nacional de Bellas Artes
in Havana Cuba and wishing I could remember exactly
(while examining the extensive collection of Greek vases
the Titians the self-portrait of Sir Joshua Reynolds
the paintings showing Negroes in foolish situations)
what Greg had to say about the painters of the Revolution
many look as if they had been more inspired by Greg Curnoe
than he by them or them by anything else and I'm trying to
remember what Greg had to say about the work of

Eduardo Abela (1889–1965)
Amelia Peláez del Casal (1896–1968)
Víctor Manuel García (1897–1969)

María Pepa Lamarque (1893–?)
Mirta Cirra Herrera (1904–1986)
Jorge Arche (1905–1956)
Mariano Rodríguez Alvarez (1912–1990)
René Portocarrero (1912–1985)
Gilberto de la Nuez Iglesias (1913–?)
Servando Cabrera Moreno (1923–1981)
Angel Acosta León (1930–1964)
Manuel Mendive Hoyo (1944–?)
Gustavo Acosta Pérez (1958–?)

In every little gallery of the museum
an elderly woman snoozes on a hard-back chair
and as I enter she gets up and keeps standing
sees my camera and without my asking
gives me *carta blanca* to take all the photos I want
of whatever painting I'd like to photograph

And as I leave each little gallery
and enter the next one
the woman in the previous one sits down
and resumes her little siesta
and the one in the new one wakes up
and stands up and starts telling me
I should feel free to take pictures
all the pictures I want whatever
and she doesn't even mind if I use a flash
(though I wouldn't dream of it)

I fall in love with the paintings of Jorge Arche
and take great pains to photograph them
because no reproductions are available
nobody knows anything about Jorge Arche
I wonder if Dulce María Loynaz the poet
who is ninety-two and lives where she always lived

in a beautiful house in the Miramar section of Havana
I wonder if she knew Jorge Arche
and maybe even was in love with him
he is so handsome in his *Autorretrato* (1935)
or his *Mi Mujer y Yo* (1939)
or his *Primavero Descarso* (1940)
and his paintings are so melancholy and simple
and Dulce María Loynaz is so beautiful in the
beautiful photo taken of her in 1947
her poems are so melancholy and simple
after all she knew everyone
Federico García Lorca (1898–1936)
Juan Ramón Jiménez (1881–1958)
Gabriela Mistral (1889–1957)
she must have known Jorge Arche
no info on how Jorge Arche met his end
but he was even younger than Greg when he died
and maybe Dulce María Loynaz
was as bereft at the Death of Jorge Arche
as we all were at the Death of Greg Curnoe

And so I plan to go to the Canadian Embassy
and ask them to arrange for me to meet
Dulce María Loynaz who is in her nineties
and has beautiful long hands according to the singer
Oderay Ortega Atán who went to her house and sang for her
along with other members of the Cuban National Choir
when Señora Loynaz won the Premio Cervantes in 1992
but I get sick and stay sick
until I have to return to Toronto

And I feel as if
all the paintings Greg ever did
all the magnificent installations
all the heartbreaking watercolour sketches

all the miraculous pen and ink drawings
all the brilliant rubber-stamp canvasses
all the funny things he made both when he
was a kid and when he was all grown up
all the little rubber-stamp notebooks he made
all the photos he took
all the bicycles painted on plexiglass
so they cast a shadow like real bicycles
all the portraits of his friends
and of Sheila
Owen
Galen
Zoë
the various family dogs cats birds
the views from his studio windows
all the paintings he wanted to paint
but never got around to it

All this huge collection of stuff
follows me around wherever I go
just outside my field of vision
I can feel it there
stretching out in all directions
away from me
I can't see any of it
but I can sense it being there like space
surrounding the planet on which we briefly live —

And then on the way home I remember that Greg
had been in Havana in November 1988
at the invitation of the Cuban government
with a group of poets and painters from London Ontario
including Christopher Dewdney who said Greg seemed
very awkward in the foreign environment of Cuba
(which wasn't surprising he even seemed a little awkward

on his visits to the foreign environment of Toronto)
Greg's wife Sheila was there too and she said Greg
filled two fat notebooks with strange observations
mostly about his feeling terribly awkward in Cuba
but somehow the notebooks got lost during the trip
Greg searched everywhere for them but they were gone

And one day in Cuba Greg recovered from his
awkwardness and took a bicycle
up into the hills overlooking
the beaches east of Havana
Santa Maria del Mar for instance
and did some lovely watercolour sketches
of graceful palm trees by the sea
and these watercolours go very nicely
with his little watercolour sketches painted
along the shores of Lake Huron and Lake Erie
as I'm sure he must have realized
as he stood there painting in the hills
overlooking the beaches east of Havana
being careful not to get sunburned
wearing sunblock and a floppy straw hat
maybe feeling a little homesick
on November 17 1988 four years
minus three days before his death

DYING METAPHORS

after George Orwell

RING THE CHANGES ON.
Little Abbie Hands stood on top of Terry Fox Mountain, took the ring
off her finger and flung it over the side, then sighed. The binoculars
were the next to go and then her clothing, her little children, the dog,
the family car, the sort of thing your left hand might write all on its
own as you sit reading Iris Murdoch novels, your heart stuffed with
family photos, and somebody is staring at you through the window and
you hope it's somebody you haven't seen since grade 6.
   A man who vows to give his voice to the dreams of others.

TAKE UP THE CUDGELS FOR.
Cudgels are stout sticks used for beating the brains out of bad guys.
What is that smell? The smell of new brains being born, a train of
newborn babies steaming down the Santa Fe Trail at midnight with a
full moon and neat rows of palmettos.
   You could take one of these sticks and break all the hearts on your
block. Love is like milk, you have to keep it on ice. Shakespeare: They
that love best their loves shall not enjoy.

TOE THE LINE.
David, what are you doing? I cannot tell a lie. I am towing a lion from
here to Coeur d'Alene. And did you know there are more lions in Idaho
than Ontario?
   David, I want your heart to be open for love at all times.
   My name is Toe. I'm a line. You can call me a contemporary non-
metrical form. David is such a lovely lion-thrower but where does he
get his lions from and how does he know when to quit?
   You always quit when you least want to.

Ride Roughshod Over.

David, why don't you hop on your bike and ride over to Roughshod right away. Your mother always used to say here's a quarter, run over to the store and get me eleven cents' worth of monkey mucus and a nickel's worth of sandwich sperm — and make sure the sperm is slimy. Then I'll make you the loveliest lunch.

David's mother gets angry when we call him David. So when she's around we call him Shitface. And she's going to be around until November. David's problem is he's overly roughshod. Most people around here wear ballet slippers if anything.

Stand Shoulder to Shoulder With.

It's too late. If you really wanted to come you would have been here by now. Suddenly his face changed colour. I had a hunch he was about to hunch his shoulders, even though I knew it was almost lunchtime. When he hunched them I said I knew you were going to do that and he merely shrugged his shoulders with typical Gallic charm.

The sandblasters knew all about standing shoulder to shoulder and all that that entails. Two thats in a row. That's that.

Play into the Hands Of.

I was walking around all day down by the river with my hands cut off at midstream. I was feeling sad inside. When all at once they nabbed me for playing left wing and lopped off my lovely paws.

Don't listen to him. He just wants you to play into his hands. But he doesn't have hands. Not today maybe but you see him tomorrow and he'll have hands aplenty to torment you with.

Dear Abbie Hands, how I love to torment you. My hands these days are full of amorous purpose. One of my hands played into the other. Which reminds me: what have you done with my Swiss Army knife?

No Axe to Grind.
Suddenly I found myself facing the emptiness of a blank piece of paper and remembering what I was born for. And so I started writing and ideas flew onto the page like little black cigars.

This is the great emptiness Bodhidharma spoke of, the great well of peace alluded to by all the holy women of the past.

We have no axe to grind. Who cares if Abbie Hands is sleeping with Tom in Philadelphia tonight (gasp!)? Grind coffee, not axes.

Grist to the Mill.
You never know when you're going to upset the gods. You could be just floating along for forty years and suddenly these words appear: Grist to the mill. Two spectators were killed and six injured at the start of the Ninth Balsam River Marathon and Second World River Boat Championships.

Oh, David, come home. I want you back with me forever. I want to play dying metaphors into your hands. This is your old friend Abbie Hands speaking, smoking little black cigars and writing down by the old mill stream.

Fishing in Troubled Waters.
Don't you love the twenties? The styles, the flames licking up our spines. We were sailing along on Moonlight Bay when we heard the white folks singing these words: Fishing in troubled waters.

Boy, was I scared. There were people getting lynched all around me. Once I realized how troubled I'd been I couldn't get enough fishing in.

LOVE'S GOLDEN SPLENDOR

A woman is reading a book called *Love's Golden Splendor*
on the bus heading down to the Pape station
and I look out the window and see a young man
pushing an old lady in a wheelchair, quickly,
for it is about to start raining.
Later, on the subway, there's another woman
reading *Love's Golden Splendor*, and a young
African woman, fashionably dressed, sits by herself
unself-consciously singing Billie Holiday songs.

My verses are subtle yet unschooled, amateur but never
didactic. The twentieth century means nothing to me.
This could be ninth-century China for all I care.
Everything is myth. I've wound up all my affairs
and am about to put all my possessions in a boat
and push it out in the bay and sink it. We have never
taken a step out of eternity. I think it's time
for you to come with me. Let's just go
and let's not know or even care where we're going.

1940

In the course of ten days I recovered sufficiently from my injuries to attend school,
where, for a little while, I was looked upon as a hero, on account of having been
blown up.
— Thomas Bailey Aldrich

I wanted to write a poem about the year I was born
and I wanted to keep myself completely out of it.
I wanted to write a poem about the year I was born
as a celebration of existence in general
but I can only hope to do this successfully
out of my own self, my own particular sense
of the nature of existence, of the reason
I feel an urge to celebrate it in poetry.
To keep myself out of it would require
considerable deliberation and in my experience
poetry does not thrive on deliberation.
Poetry thrives when language is allowed to flow
naturally like a river, brook or creek
and in order to initiate and maintain that flow
the poet must stand aside, keep himself
completely out of it, and once that flow begins
should it wish to carry him or her with it
he or she should not resist. In order
to write poetry one must keep himself out of it
but once the poetry begins it soon becomes apparent
it has a mind of its own and if it wants
to exploit intimate aspects of the poet's life
to resist it would be to destroy it.
For poetry thrives on naturalness
and naturalness thrives on intimacy
and in a world so horrendously inhuman
that even intimacy seems on the verge of extinction
the most intimate poetry will be the most loved

at least by the few who sense most fully
the gravity of our impending loss.
The poet who tries to keep his own form
out of poetry is faced with a formal problem
but the problem tends to trivialize itself
when faced with the primal force of the poem
and when the poet's form fades and vanishes
all nature becomes alive and flows
into the poem and adopts any form it wants
including the poet's and if it wants
it will turn the poet inside out.
The most masculine man must occasionally long
to become for a brief period at least
the most feminine woman, to feel
in the height of passion all that beauty
from the other side, as the most
civilized human must occasionally long
to experience that formless light
of nature, to hear that universal voice
more loving than a perfect mother
instructing each cell how to grow
unimpeded by the superego.
The poet who strives to keep out of the poem
finds himself in everything
as when I hear of someone born in 1940
I feel a sense of kinship
that grows into a kind of intimacy
in which the merest touch of fingers
brings a sense of nature's unity.

I thought I'd go to the newspaper morgue
and read up on 1940. But then I thought
about the spirit of poetry and what it
would have thought about that idea.
Not much, I thought. I felt a little

nervous and so I had a glass of milk.
I thought about my mother and father
in their early twenties, making love
in a small house in the east end
of Hamilton, Ontario, the country at war.
I remember a photo of my mother holding me.
It must have been Christmas 1940.
Her eyes were shining, mine closed
with inexpressible delights.
Perhaps that intimacy, the memory of it
we all share, is the key, that keeps
something in us pointed forever
at our birthplace, as if some magic
magnetic stone were buried beneath it.
And Britain, where every place
is a birthplace a thousand times over,
was being attacked from the air
and the endless holocaust doesn't enter
my poetry easily and my poetry
must always be easy or it's not poetry.
I know when it's not poetry. Who doesn't
know the difference between a river
sweetly pouring the heavens to the sea
and a canal?
               I wanted
to write a poem about the year I was born.
I wanted to write a poem for every year of my life
and call them *The Annual Odes* although I know
that even if I composed four a year I wouldn't
be caught up until I was almost fifty
and I knew I would have trouble with 1941
and the whole thing smacks of excess ambition
and over-deliberation, contrary to the core
of the spirit of poetry into which I do not want
to force my way but only to be absorbed cell by cell

if at all although I suppose we've all been there
from the start and never really knew it
except insofar as we think we have.

I wanted to write a poem about the year I was born.
It was late at night, far past midnight,
the mysterious time for writing mysterious poems.
I was getting sleepy when I started and now my god
I'm really tired. It's 2:30!

Maybe one last line will come.
Shall I continue downstream?
Now I'm really talking to myself.
Is this intimacy? This is not a poem
about the birth of a poem. This is a poem
composed shortly after the birth of something else
or during the birth of something else to be exact.
I don't know what to call it but there is nothing
abstract about it although it has never been named
successfully. I know I'm not the only one to have
seen it but there has been little agreement
as to its qualities, attributes, shape
or even its colour.
                        I think it's white
with little black letters all over it
(like the hat in "A Form of Passion")
and it's unspeakably intelligent.

To give birth to it is to know everything.
I wanted to write a poem about repetition.
I wanted to celebrate existence as if I knew
anything about existence except that at bottom
there is something that can only be celebrated.

The fashions of 1940, the deaths, the agony.
Why am I sitting here writing like this
feeling as if my face and hands and feet and
legs and arms form a piece of music
of indeterminate length
that came out of the musical earth
like a bubble?

And the world would be more peaceful
if I fell asleep
and the earth would be more musical
if I fell asleep.
        I have a name
for sleep. I call it Thomas.
Some call it Slumber. Some call it
Sleeping Bag. I could call it Elizabeth
but I prefer to call it Thomas.
You gotta have a name.
Hello, Thomas!

THE SEARCHLIGHT

He was well groomed and well dressed
and he stopped me on the street
and asked for a quarter.

When I gave him one he said:

I can draw power
from the ground
up through my legs
to make my heart
shine like a searchlight.

KITSILANO BEACH ON A MAY EVENING

If you told them you wanted to be a fireman someday
they'd let you in to watch the big game on television
at the Kenilworth Avenue firehall in 1954
and you'd ride your bicycle along the Pipe Line
past the row of wooden posts painted green and see
the blossoming pear tree in her backyard and she'd
be there, sunning, reading *The Old Man and the Sea*,
on the back-porch roof, in her green bikini.

When does the possibility of taking one's own life
first appear? You'd ask for her brother,
a few years older, long wavy blond hair, blue eyes
that never seemed to look at you or anyone.
And she'd say he's gone, gone to Hollywood
to be a movie star, and you'd say you'd seen a movie
and the star reminded you of her, and she'd say
she hated that movie and was insulted that you
thought she resembled such a third-rate actress
and she was pink in the spring, brown in the summer,
grey in the fall and white in the winter,
Ruth was her name, hair the colour of daffodils,
and nothing came of your desire to befriend her.
Years later you heard she'd been convicted of stealing
money from the bank where she worked as a teller
and giving it to her boyfriend to buy heroin.

And you remember the night when you were eight.
You'd just finished reading *Peter Pan* for the eighth time
and for the eighth time felt a wave of embarrassment.
There was a pregnant woman walking by under the streetlamps.
You punched her in the stomach full force and ran home.
And the time your friend Bobby Zambori
in short pants was sitting on the front step,

your dad scraping the house for paint.
You held the tip of a screwdriver in the flame
of the blowtorch for several minutes
then touched it to Bobby's bare leg.

You've always been psychotic. You always look
as if you've just finished strangling a cat.
Just last year you deserted your wife and children
with particular cruelty. You enjoy thinking about it.
And you're glad you thought to put on a sweater
on this cool spring evening in the strange orange light
of Kitsilano Beach, your slow lazy breathing
cooling your heart's excessive heat.

Lonely men stroll by and glance at you. They are wondering
what you're thinking, walking so slow. Two mallards
float by on the oil-slicked swells of English Bay. A young
blond woman sits on a bench under a light. She is reading
The Old Man and the Sea. Several freighters
are moored farther out. Dozens of grapefruit
bob up and down in the water. Maybe they've fallen
from one of the boats. Maybe they're full of heroin!
The lights and outline of a large sailboat sailing slowly
in towards False Creek Mouth remind you of wealth and poverty.
The old steam locomotive in the park reminds you of Chiang's
soldiers who used to take captives and shove them live
down the chimneys of locomotives like this, down into
the steam chamber full of boiling water.

Suddenly you hear a scream, a girl's voice.
She yells out "No!" as if she really means it.
It seems to have come from the dark area behind the
tennis courts and you search through clumps of trees
and find nothing. Don't bother calling a cop.
They'd never take you seriously. Besides,

how do you know you didn't imagine the voice?
Don't you still sometimes hear your mother calling you?

Remember that photo you sent your mother last year?
You wrote on the back here's the nicest person in the world
saying hello to all the other nice people in the world.
And of course you meant it, even though now
you've taken to warning people what a rotten bastard you are,
how you love to betray people when they've finally
yielded their absolute vulnerability, how you'd be shot
in wartime and probably will be even in peacetime.
You wouldn't last a day in Belfast or Beirut.

And then you begin to preen, speaking in the most
superficial Jungian terms of the shadow's integration
and when your naïve audience asks what you do with it
once it's integrated you say you keep your eye on it
like a lama measuring his breathing in and out
for once you're aware of your capacity for monstrosity
you're less likely to destroy yourself and others
and all you want to do is live in peace, by yourself,
adding nothing to the misery of the world.
That black hum over there is Stanley Park.
That incongruous constellation of stars is the illuminated
Grouse Mountain ski lift. Two men are standing
on the breakwater scooping the grapefruit with butterfly nets.
Everything that ever was is in the air tonight.
On the horizon, tugboat operators are getting drunk.

With a tender smile you draw Ruth towards you and touch
your lips to her forehead so impossibly chaste and lovely.
She is wearing nothing but a loincloth.
She is fourteen forever.

ORCHARD SUITE

I

Miles & miles of fruit trees
  have been chopped down
to build these houses, each one
  full of happy children.

II

  Ladies & gentlemen: The word for the deity of whom I have heard
so much throughout my long childhood years at Sunday School could
start with no other letter than "G."

III

  There is a hole in the centre of my heart through which God can
be seen. Out of Him through that hole Creation has spilled.

IV

  It is now impossible to get away with making the same speech in
every town. One must be completely open or completely shut.

V

  When I press a certain spot on my chest I am filled with joy.

VI

  The neck of my stomach is directly behind the level of the bottom
of my rib cage.

VII

I offend most people with my niceness. Occasionally, however, I
deeply annoy someone with my rottenness. There seems to be no
happy medium for this happy medium. Perhaps my niceness is an effort
to compensate for my thorough rottenness. But then really who cares?
Why should I care?

VIII

Boy, he really knew himself!

IX

In my head
Is my heart,
I am dead
In my art.

X

Discuss the blind in pictures.

STRANGE LANGUAGE

Language is a breakwater causing the blind
Waves of the mind suddenly to halt
And explode. Anonymity's universal.
A man in a grimy section of Miami
Walks around with a placard proclaiming:
"*I'm* employed! *I* work for God!"

Wonderful to watch the dolphins leaping
In the crashing waves off Key West
Yet I'm so sad I find it hard
To be around me half the time.
Microscopic cells in the bloodstream
Bump into each other and say: "Excuse me,
Don't know your name but we sure are wet."

I'm wearing my windbreaker, standing on the breakwater,
Breaking wind, passing water,
Watching the rise and fall of the anonymous
Waves. Hard to know what to say
At times like this. Is there anything
I can do? You could be my mother.
I could watch over you as you gave birth to me,
I could hold your hand and watch you die.
I could tell everyone of your courage under fire,
Your primal dignity. How you fought your terror
And how you knew when to surrender.

Like characters in an opera we're trapped in our own
Broken hearts so distraught
They'll never beat wildly again, they'll just rot.

We're watching television, Kelly Gruber at bat.
Mother says, "Look, he wants to shake
Hands with all the other guys."
"But they won't shake with him," I say.

I'm a mile out in Lake Erie
And mother is calling me in for lunch.
She's forever bursting into tears,
Throwing her arms around me and saying:
"David, why are you so sad?
Don't you know I've always loved you?"

Gruber hit the ball out of the park
And got to shake hands with all his teammates.
So that was what mother was talking about.
"Why has that little boy got his mouth open?"
She said when the standings came on the screen.
Mother had a way of turning everyone she knew
Into a Zen Buddhist with koans like that.
She'd die before I'd get the answer.

I'm holding a cup of coffee and she says:
"You could make it go if you wanted to."
She looks at me, bursts into tears
And says: "Oh David, you've broken your heart."
New moon rising at the eastern end of Wellesley.
Penetrating silence when I ask my mother
If I was easier to raise than my brother.

A matador is gored by a horn,
Someone dies, someone's born.
Whenever I see a woman pregnant
I think of my mother being born again.
For most of us the only way
To become a lion is to be devoured by one.
Body of a lamb, soul of a lion.

From now on men will have the souls
Of women and women men as well.
You keep thinking there must be a way
Of bringing the beloved back to life.
The magic word and they'll sit right up
In their coffin and say: "You need a haircut."
Just to hear their strange language again.

FRANK O'HARA

It was the high school orchestra. We raised money
by selling aluminum clothes-peg boxes.
On the side of each was a red emblem.
I think it said REALISTIC.
You can check it out. There are still some
nailed to posts in the east end of Hamilton, Ontario.
And with the money we went on an Easter field trip
to New York.
The music teacher
Bernard Blades
fell in love with the string-bass player
Lois Lawrence.
She must have been sixteen.
He left his wife and kids
and married her.
Actually he stole her away from the trombone player
who was also sixteen.
This kind of thing never happens in *Archie*.
The trombone player I met years later
and he told me that Mr. Blades and Lois
had been very happy
for a while
and had a couple of kids of their own
but in her early thirties Lois got cancer
and died
and two weeks later Mr. Blades had a heart attack
and died.
I thought the trombone player sounded a little smug,
as if he were happy the way it turned out.
He belonged to one of those funny religions.

Meanwhile, back in New York, I didn't want to go
to the United Nations building
so I sneaked off to the Museum of Modern Art
which wasn't on our itinerary
and got into a long interesting conversation
with the man at the Information Counter.
He was so nice to me and he took me for a Coke
and paid for it himself
and he knew all about poetry and art
and he even said Jack Kerouac and Allen Ginsberg
were friends of his
and he told me it was very important never to let yourself
get bored by poetry
if you wanted to keep writing
and he advised me to stay in Canada
and give up my desire
to move to New York when I turned eighteen.
Years later I read the poetry of Frank O'Hara
and when I saw his picture
I knew
that's who it had been.

And now Frank too
along with Mr. Blades and Lois
is dead
but I bet Frank at any rate
is not bored
not even by this poem.
Are you, Frank?

VISIONS OF OLD HAMILTON

I

Through the sky drifted a yellow balloon, a large illuminated cross
    hanging from its basket, & it seemed to be following Major Bate-
    man as he ran, cape flowing behind him, through the streets of old
    Hamilton.
Suspended with tiny pebbles, the large dark waves of the bay received
    him as he ran off the dock at the foot of James Street.
Curse you, curse you! He shook his fist at the balloon as he fished
    himself out of the water, rubbed the tiny pebbles from his eyes &
    wrung out the cape.
Subdued but still angry, Major Bateman stormed back to his office,
    occasionally looking over his shoulder & spitting an ugly oath at
    the softly following balloon.

II

The major finally succeeded in creating fish in his old laboratory over
    the pool room at Balmoral & Cannon,
a little school of about 12, all different colours,
& he was hurrying down to the bay to dump them in before they died.
He bicycled on the boardwalk because the roads were so muddy.
He passed two old friends who were out of work & looking for
    handouts —
The major thought he better hang on to the money he had, it might
    come in handy,
he never even considered giving them the fish. He rode out on the dock
at the foot of James Street & dumped in the fish.
The fish looked up at him through the clear waters & smiled
& each fish had a silver dollar in its mouth
& there were stacks of $500 bills floating slowly
out from under the dock like miraculous little rafts.

III

Major Bateman lifted the manhole cover at the corner of Kenilworth &
   Britannia.
The water flowing through the sewer was unusually clear. Through it he
   could see
huge ugly blind prehistoric fish, dozens of them, each one obviously
   capable of devouring a full-grown man,
but at the bottom of the sewer, sparkling like memories of childhood,
were dozens of huge coins. Characteristically, Major Bateman didn't
   hesitate.
He dived in.

MY MOTHER IN HISTORY

My mother wants me to have a lover
So I told her about you. I said you were rich,
Beautiful, intelligent,
Aristocratic, and mother said:
"Oh heck, why don't you give her a chance?"

In the humblest poem the proudest sentiment.
    Until when was the coelecanth
        Extinct? *No one knows for sure*
           But it was believed to be extinct
              Until 1938.
                I came out of the poet's head
           And am now wrapped around the cap
      Of his toothpaste. What am I?
A hair. What makes light work?
Many hands. And so on....

Mother gave me when I went to
    Transylvania last year
        Her camera and asked me to take
           Pictures of horses and churches for her.
    I also took pictures of the towns
Where her mother and father were born.

Neither of which she had ever visited.
But when I got home and had the pictures
Printed, the only one she took
An interest in was the one of her granddaughter
Wearing a wide-brimmed straw hat and stepping
Proudly from the train at Alba Iulia.

When I was a kid I complained to Uncle Joe
That mother wouldn't let me read *For Whom the Bell Tolls*.
So Joe ordered pink roses in a bouquet
With a card: "Let the kid read it. Hemingway."

Of course she complied. She was only sixteen
Years younger than Papa and one younger than Dada.
Mother in history: Born a hundred years after
The death of Jane Austen, twenty-four before me.

PARENTHOOD

Everyone wants to outlive his parents.
Parents with dignity as overpowering
As that of the servant in *The Big Sleep*.
But nobody wants to outlive his children.
The servant who says to Humphrey Bogart:
"I make *many* mistakes, Mr. Marlowe."

A child's a mistake you're glad you made
Though he or she has to suffer and die.
Five billion children in the world
But none's as wonderful as your own,
None as deserving of a life free of pain.

I want to live to be so old and wise
My children will forget my imperfections.
Early years of disappointment and grief,
Cruel absence, duty's derelictions,
Bizarre and insensitive errors in judgement.

Such a coward, I can't bear to think
     Of their deaths, unless they're old and wise
          And the final gong has flushed me out
               Of this amazing maze in which we're trapped.
                    The flare of the soul's SOS.
               Children are born, the world develops
          Points and edges never noticed before.
Mindlessness makes way for sentimental menace.

If you die first I'll be strong.
Nobody likes a wimpy dad.
The occasional tear to show you're sincere
Seems to be all that's really required.
If I die before your last sigh
You can think of me as that silly guy
Who had no way of dealing with all his love.

CHILD MOLESTERS

I am shipping these books to you collect.
I picked up a box & the books fit perfectly.
It was just the right size.
There are no more books.

Perhaps what I am writing now
will someday be in a book
that you will want to have

for there are mysterious people in the world
who steal children & kill them
& stuff them in holes in the ground

& I wonder if they cackle with glee
as they stir drops of blood into their drinks.

We are small people compared to the distances
that separate us
but we are surrounded by books
I with yours & you with mine

each little book trying to reject
the themes of all the others.

A man got out of his red truck and opened
a door in the bottom of a red box at the roadside.
It was a letter box and he dumped the letters
into a bag and threw them into the truck.
The letters have all been sorted & delivered
to their destinations all over the world
by now, but it is still in my mind,
the emptying of the box,
the red truck moving on to the next box.

EARLY AUTUMN GUITAR

Another wasted night, the full moon blurred through thin wet clouds,
and I'm trying both to forget you and not forget you at the same time.
Although little in these poems is what it seems to be, I've graduated
from irony to ambiguity in the length of time it takes to do so (longer
than it takes to string a guitar, not as long as it takes to learn to play one).
My attempts to extricate you from my heart seem cowardly, my desire to
keep my memories of you fresh and constant foolishly courageous. This
is not what I thought life would be like, but the moon though dimmed
has never seemed so close, whispering to me of serenity, faithfulness
and endless renewal. Perhaps this has nothing to do with you, this is
my attempt to use a dilemma of my own creation to breathe fresh music
into my mind as you revivify yourself with your secret late-night calls.
They say the soul secretly seeks out sadness to bring itself to life, to
remind its creatures of its own unwavering divinity, and if this is so I
must be on the verge of a great awakening. Only the creatures are judged
to be different, not the soul that animates them from within, and perhaps
only through this awakening will we be able to find ourselves together
once again, invisibly but indivisibly. Gypsy guitars accompany me
on my nightly solitary strolls through the early autumn avenues, I am
alone one moment and flooded with your invisible presence the next,
quietly, the quietness I felt in you, strongly, the strength I felt in you,
helplessly, the helplessness I loved in you, beautifully, the crazy beauty
you brought me and its sanity. Yet these rapturous nights appear and are
    lost,
the world loses all its value, becomes a cosmic garbage dump, the world
has nothing to offer true lovers but the great emancipation of death, the
    death
that comes whenever you think of it, the long-trapped energy of life
suddenly and ecstatically free. Friends wonder at my lack of desire
and since I don't wish to alarm them I start new projects until I'm
back on track with people to meet, articles to write, classes to teach,
contracts to sign, and I go on crazy little spending sprees, a new
wardrobe, expensive electronic gadgetry, and I take all this new stuff

home and unwrap it and say hello darling to each new thing I unwrap.
And everything's all right except I'm doing all these things without a
sense of expectation, nothing is going to come from all of this, the world
has nothing to offer, but I am burning again and suddenly I see there are
certain tasks only I can perform, certain modest problems only I can solve.

Words are tropical fish that disport and distort themselves beneath the
    surface.
And so I swim in a pool of thick warm words and at night dream of
    wondrous
pigmented sentences lying in tubes waiting to be uncapped and squeezed.
Every word I write will have to be cancelled and I hope it can be by me.
Yet there is a Great Word from which all words come and that word is the
unspeakable word that means you-at-rest-in-my-soul-and-I-in-yours.

A REPRESENTATIVE OF VIOLENCE

Sunday afternoon in early April
the cat purring at my feet in hunger
no food in the house & Joan groaning
& the two kids looking at me

my stomach & head full of beer
    on this day of spring
    with tulips green tips protruding
    & some people buy artificial tulips
    & stick them upright in their beds
    like politicians who pretend
    they have a heart & give a damn

    & I'm about to float out to my car
    & slide through sober traffic to
    pick up a batch of hot food

    What'll it be? Teenburgers from the A&W?
    (which stands for Amburgers & Wootbeer)
    or Chinese food from Roy's
    or Italian grub from Vista's?
    I wonder as I hop in car & can't decide
    & the car veers straight towards Vista's.

    I order three chicken noodle soups
    one small pizza double cheese
    one bag of lasagna double hot
    & the girl's sweater it's so tight
    & her red hair & plucked eyebrows
    & her plumpness so overbound!

    Waiting, I pull out of my pocket
    my copy of *The Double Helix*

& coming in past me the people
　　eager for hot food overprepared
　　& going out past me the sated
　　newly amazed by the colours
　　of a spring afternoon, early spring
　　in the unbombed cities of the Great Lakes.

MY BODY WAS EATEN BY DOGS

I met her while walking in Egypt
on the road to Oxyrhynchus
where the Ibycus papyrus was found.
Her body had been eaten by dogs,
torn into little pieces,
each piece
        still glowing with life.

How I met her, I tripped on the road
then noticed the rock that caught my toe
was a face,
        a large broken nose and a
        once-smooth chin cracked and chipped.

She looked up at me with hardened eyes
silently pleading to be picked up

and I wondered what it would be like
to spend centuries without a workable body,
life clinging to small fragments of petrified flesh
like reflections to pieces of shattered glass.

And there she was lying like a rock
in the road, helpless, a living
rock among all the other rocks,
a living planet searching the heavens
for signs of life.

And finally as I hesitated wondering
if I had time to waste on this, this ...
I mean it was a curious situation all right
but the landscape was loaded, overloaded
with equally curious situations
and I was in a hurry to reach the sea

and the strange black mouth opened
and I had a glimpse of the awful warmth
of a life that has nothing else
but warmth.

My body, she said,
was eaten by dogs.

And her mouth slowly closed again
like a clam with a morsel to digest
and she continued staring up at me
as if I were the first person
in five thousand years
to have noticed her lying on the road

and I picked her up
and put her in my bag
and eventually brought her back to Canada

and now she is sitting on my bookshelf
in my log cabin in Tuktoyaktuk
and every nine minutes or so
she opens her mouth to say
My body was eaten by dogs

and her shrunken blue-grey eyes
never close.

THE PORTABLE NIETZSCHE

November 15, 1969

In the end I would much rather be a Basel professor than God.
— Nietzsche's last note, Jan. 6, 1889

The city swallows the day daily, shudders & forgets.

I first met Bill Davies in 1956, he was 29, an ex-alcoholic.
He was proprietor of the L(ewd) & V(ulgar) Variety at King William &
    Mary
southeast corner, it's now a municipal parking lot.

I entered the store & asked for an orange Popsicle.
My friend Wayne McPherson played the pinball machine.
There was an indoor phone booth like in old-fashioned drugstores
there was a huge magazine & book rack behind the pinballs
there were stacks of new hardbound books around the front of the counter
canned goods, bread, cakes, pop coolers, what a mess that place was!
Huge towering piles of old papers & cardboard cartons.

When Bill handed me the Popsicle I noticed he was looking at me!
He watched my hands as I broke open the Popsicle
& watched my tongue as I licked it. I could tell he was watching closely
despite his severely cross-eyed condition.

I asked him if that was his grey Jaguar XK120 parked outside.

He started telling me all about carburetors & power slides,
told me about driving all the way to Port Elgin in 2nd gear.
I asked him why he'd want to go to Port Elgin & he laughed,
his eyeballs flipping around like pinballs, hair sticking out in clumps,
little broken black stumps of teeth.

I didn't ask about the Portable Nietzsche on the rear window ledge of the
    Jag.
I left the store without paying for the Popsicle & didn't return for 3 years.

I heard a lot of strange stories about Bill, he was the son
of a high-up Dofasco executive, had 4 older sisters,
became a hopeless drunk in his early & mid-twenties
losing jobs constantly, smashing up cars, in & out of jail,
busted for turning cartwheels, bellowing Shakespeare,
singing dirty songs & laughing loud in public
(this was Ontario in the 1950s) & old drunks I talk to now
who knew him then claimed he was *psychic*,
used to make their hair stand on end with uncanny
but trivial predictions & he couldn't get this power
working right at crap games or at the races.

Then he started to practise Yoga after long series of religious visions &
    ecstatic drunken glimpses
& his Aunt Edna provided him with the Variety Store.

I used to walk by the store & look at the book display in the window.
Books on motorsport mainly & sometimes I would notice the books on
    Yoga,
Yogananda's *Autobiography of a Yogi*, *Zen Telegrams*, Pound's *Cantos*,
William Carlos Williams.

In 1959 I wrote some poems & in October I took them to Bill.
Just walked in, said Remember me? Here's the 5¢ for the 1956 Popsicle,
what do you think of these poems?

He told me to send the poems to City Lights in San Francisco
& wrote me a letter of introduction, actually he was going to send them
    himself,
the letter he wrote to Lawrence Ferlinghetti, said what Ginsberg &
    Whitman
had done for the United States, & Blake & Wordsworth did for England,
young McFadden here is doing for Canada. Poor Bill so lonely.
He provided the envelope, addressed it, all I had to do was
stamp it & mail it but I didn't, far too proud.

The store was diagonally across from Central Police Station.
Robert Downing the sculptor was a Hamilton cop in those days
& he wrote a book of poems, typed them out in neat carbons
about 5 copies stapled into 5 little books & one he gave to Bill
heroically inscribed. Stuff like (I paraphrase)
"'Tis better to build a window than to knock down a wall."
I really liked Bob even though he was a cop,
he used to lend me his car, see how sculptors get their start?

Nobody was buying anything but books from Bill's store
so he decided to specialize in books & moved to a little shop
half a block east on the north side (143) of King William
the shop's still standing, it had been a Salvation Army clothing store
& now is a camera supply shop. When Bill moved in there he
became the centre of some kind of strange circle
that got to be too much for him. He
loved it & hated it & schemed for escape.

He was a good talker, a good listener,
& hellish good at instant psychotherapy.
If you needed a Zen master you just went to Bill.
Long queues of people with long tales of woe,
didn't sell many books.

Then he sold the bookstore & started giving Yoga classes
& lay psychotherapeutic sessions at a new place
23 Augusta.
        He got his teeth fixed, somehow corrected his eye
& became a handsome 40. He married a girl about 20
& they had a baby boy.
        Early this year I visited Bill
& noted new strains of bitterness, coming down hard on fellow Yogis
like Swami Vishnudevananda, Tim Leary, Lobsang Rampa.

This summer he had a heart attack without realizing it.
I still haven't got this figured out. The attack wasn't massive
& he didn't feel it & it was 10 days before what he thought was bronchitis
drove him to the doctor who diagnosed the heart condition correctly
& slapped him in the hospital.

        He was out in 6 weeks or so
then weakened & went back in then got out again, claiming
because he was a Yogi the medicine had the opposite effect.
He was strong enough to walk around the block
but he weakened again this time severely with lungs & liver
filling with water, Bill weakly screaming for Ginger Ale
(Canada Dry has a bite to it but Niagara Dry'd do) which was forbidden.
I figured a bottle'd do more good than harm in the sense that it would
relax him, he'd never be relaxed enough for any recovery with every cell
screaming for Ginger Ale so I smuggled in to him a small cold Canada Dry
& helped him to sit up so he could drink it, just skin & bones,
& as soon as he started to drink it we could hear his wife coming upstairs

so he had to sip fast, sad-eyed sipper, & later when I asked how he'd
    enjoyed it
he said, "I … had to … drink too … fast."

                                        Now he's back in hospital again,
Intensive Care Ward, they give Ginger Ale but his craving is over.

It's been 6 months since the attack & his condition is worse than ever.

Tonight talking to Jackie on the phone (Bill's wife)
& she says she's moving out of 23 Augusta
into a smaller apartment
                        & she'll be going to Teacher's College in September
as she couldn't bear returning to her old job as medical lab worker
it was such dry academic work but she was a dry academic person in those
    days
she says but no longer.

THE ENGLISH SHEEP DOG

Tonight in this peaceful rural home
just outside Vankleek Hill Ontario
halfway between Hawkesbury and Alexandria
I feel I must be the only one awake
in three counties except for a dog
I heard bark in the distance an hour ago.

Do you ever have those moments
when you think your brain will explode
like a rusty old twelve-gauge shotgun?
I'm thinking of the kind of man
who can calmly point a gun and fire
at a defenceless human conceived in love
and there is no shortage of such men
in this, my only century.

For yesterday my friend Rod
placed an empty plastic milk jug on a tree
and handed me his twelve-gauge shotgun
and said, "See if you can hit it."

And I, normally afraid of guns,
and having avoided both ends all my life,
checked behind the tree to make sure
there were no dogs or children
or other juicy tender things
and pulled the trigger.

The blast almost knocked me on my ass
but it was even harder on the milk jug
which just disappeared
as if it had never existed
just as if time had automatically
erased an error.

At close range
it would be more humane
than the sharpest kosher knife
and Rod said when his dogs get sick
he just shoots them, saves
on vets' bills

and Louise
who is taking courses in Yoga and Meditation
says she doesn't like twelve-gauge shotguns
and she wishes Rod would keep it out of the house
for every night he leaves it fully loaded
propped against the television set.

But there would be no pain
of that I'm sure
and Rod said, "I don't even think
you'd see a light."

And moments after I wrote those last two lines
I looked up and saw a full-grown English sheep dog
looking in the window at me, a fellow beast

and the sky began to lighten
and the birds began to sing
and I stopped writing, knowing
I hadn't got to what I meant to say.

STANDING INVITATION

We're as important as flakes
of stale tobacco in an old cigar tube
as we inch through the Northern Ontario
wilderness in a train two hours late

in fact too late even for the white
rabbit whose snowshoe prints
seem about two hours old
running alongside the track

and *whoosh* there's a bull moose
a cow and two calves licking the plump
mushrooms of snow on the outstretched
spruce boughs as if treating themselves
to a round of ice cream cones

and the woods become human

and I practise looking at the trees
with the eyes of various familiar painters
and the trees practise being blown
past the windows of the train

and the hills lose their flatness
as if painted, as if dead
and open up like hands

and the trees lose their sameness
and begin talking, gesturing, embracing,
they become much more active socially
than I ever would have thought possible
each with his or her close and distant
relatives and friends and neighbours and then
they notice me noticing them as individuals

and they seem genuinely flattered and I
am genuinely flattered in return.

They want me to visit them,
stay as long as I want.
They give me a standing
invitation.

THE COOLING SPELL

I

For millennia, it's said,
morticians have practised necrophilia
a practise perhaps rich with mysteries
the uninitiated cannot comprehend.

Although I live in the bloodiest
of centuries I can recall seeing
only one truly attractive corpse.

It was morning, she was late, she hadn't
had her coffee, she was riding her bicycle
in heavy traffic and was struck by a truck.

By the time I happened to see her,
being wheeled into the morgue,
she was turning grey. She was said
to be fifteen but she seemed to possess a
maturity most fifteen-year-olds don't display.

I was powerfully drawn to her.
For a moment I wanted to lie down beside her
on the cold slab and let my metabolism
slow down, slow down, slow down …

She looked so beautiful!

She could not have looked
more lovely alive …

II

A long, long piece of silver wire
ignored by nervous hasty passersby
ran along the sidewalk of a
  busy downtown street
in Hamilton Ontario.

Curious and with time on my hands
I followed it along among the throng.
It went on for blocks and blocks
and I became more and more curious
until finally I followed it through
the main entrance of the Iroquois Hotel
and saw it was attached
to a silver ring on the finger
of an old guy sitting there drinking beer
and staring off into empty space.

One part of me wanted to sit down with him,
buy him beer, engage him in conversation,
but I knew I wouldn't be able to drag out of him
the truth about the secret wire

in fact he probably didn't know about it
and my questions might so disturb him
they'd make it disappear.

Such things happen, I know …

And so I left the pub and followed the wire
the other way to see what was on the other end
and I followed it way past the spot where I'd first
noticed it and on and on for several more blocks
and finally right up to the ordinary-looking door
leading down into the city morgue.

I went through the door and followed the wire
down the stairs to the slab room.
The wire led up to one of the bodies.
I zipped up my jacket and pulled back the sheet.
The wire was attached to a silver ring
around the corpse's penis.

And the corpse closely resembled
the guy drinking beer in the Iroquois Hotel.

A FATHER FLIRTS WITH HIS DAUGHTER

"Here, I want you to have this,"
Said the lady with straw in her hair
At the corner of Bloor Street and Walmer Road.
And she handed me three two-dollar bills
In such a way I couldn't say no.
Fortunately there were three fellows
Begging quarters by the doughnut shop.
"Fellows," I said, "it's your lucky day."
And I handed them each a two-dollar bill.

I'd seen these guys the day before
Trying to drink Jell-O from small glass bowls.
One was a screamer specializing
In Hitler, Stalin and electroshock.
One needed money because he had lost
His wife and children at Ontario Place.
"Even a penny would do," the third
Would sing on street corners all over town.

They each grabbed a deuce and looked surprised.
"See that lady over there?" I said.
They looked at her and she looked back
And everyone smiled in the lovely moment.
"She gave me the money but I don't need it,
Because, fellows, I'm almost rich!"
Everyone looked happy for me.

So a few days later I find in the weeds
On the north side of Wellesley just west of Church
A little bundle of money: three twos
Enfolded in a five-dollar bill.
Welcome to the Great Barrier Reef.
That straw-haired lady or her spirit

Wants me to have three two-dollar bills
But I don't want them. Here, they're yours,
And the five as well, my darling daughter.

You never write and seldom call
But when you speak, your heart talks.
Last summer in Transylvania you told me:
"We'll probably be travellers for the rest of our lives
And we'll always be meeting unexpectedly
In exotic places all over the world —
Unlike Ingrid and Liv in *Autumn Sonata*....
We're alike, we'll always have
All the money we really need."

It's true I'm not very well off
But I feel richer than Boris Karloff
Because I'm a poet, because I know you
And because I know how much I need
Which isn't much but it's easy to bluff
That you have enough when you have the freedom
To know pretty well when enough is enough.

CRAZY BUS

Here I am again
on the Cannon Street bus
twenty-five years later
it's crowded
and I'm a man
full-grown
as I knew I would be
someday
not knowing where he's going
but knowing it'll come to him
when he gets there

In front of me
is Stan Sato
the saxophonist
someone I haven't seen
for twenty years
and behind me
is my landlady
someone I didn't know
twenty years ago
and across from me
is this girl from high school
I can't remember her name
maybe I never knew it
I don't even remember
ever wanting to know it
or wanting to know her
but I must have been in love with her
and didn't know it
because here she is again
on the crazy bus
and some music

comes over the loudspeaker
Muzak you know
and she starts humming along
and then singing
and her pitch is perfect
and she's not singing loudly
but her voice carries
right to me
and right through me
and I see
she knows all the words
perfectly
and seems happy
a rare thing
and that's all I wanted
to know
I guess

And out the window
it's some kind of celebration
a guy gets into a plane
and takes off
and flies around
and it's amazing
because it's an old plane
a piece of junk
from a couple of wars ago
and it has no tail
and parts of the wing
are missing
and there's a big
green garbage bag
over the windshield
blocking the pilot's view
and at the front

of the bus
some women
are arguing
about the pilot
some say he's a rat
others say he's great
they seem to know him
personally
and he has an arm missing
or a leg

And the plane's bouncing
around up there
he's having trouble
so he brings it in
and just as he touches down
the plane explodes
which doesn't surprise me
because every time
I look at a plane
it crashes
or explodes
and just as the bus goes by
the plane goes up
in a ball of fire
and you just know
the guy is dead
and the women
at the front of the bus
start crying
and they get off the bus
and walk over to the plane
or what's left of it

And the bus goes on
and it stops at the stadium
and I see a football game
is ready to start
and I remember
that's where I'm going
and I just know
whoever I root for
will win
and Stan Sato gets off
and says come on Dave
and then I get off
and then my landlady
gets off
and says wait up Dave
and we walk towards the stadium
I have a guard in front
and a guard in back
guardian angels you might say
and I can still hear that girl
singing on the bus.

SAD OLD NOTEBOOKS

Do those we remember remember us?
(Looking at notebooks from years previous.)

An oil slick swallows Labrador
With memories never remembered before.
Where do these things come from?
Nootka woman works as a dental
Assistant in Nanaimo. Teaches me backgammon
On the bus to Port Alberni. Says
I'm the fastest student she's ever had.

Fast maybe but not all that retentive.
I had no idea I was young and stupid.

Must have faith that the things we forget
Are not important for our survival.
I tell her I don't want her to think
I'm just another dim-witted white man.
Driver's listening, says he's so dumb
He couldn't find Gold River last week.
Says he was the only one in grade 5
To shave. Did all the others have beards?
She was an Ittattsoo Nootka and her name
Was Mochtiski, but everyone even her mother
Called her something like Mary Jane.

· "Chewing gum really hard" in one dialect
Means "having diarrhea" in another.
The unknown is our friend, I write.
Every atom in our body is washed with light.
This is a pleasant world. Where
Are all the mountains? Behind the fog.

Little bullet-like hailstones plunging
Out of the sky and into the sea.
Driver's wife dying of cancer.
He says he's so lucky (suicide
Runs in his family) that he can support
His family without having to sell his soul
And his wife's death is his punishment
For thinking that way or being that lucky.
Is it superstitious to think you'll be punished
For being superstitious? The driver says
He works hard to keep his temper in check.

West-coast mystique: bare feet and sandals
With bullets of hail falling into the sea.
Strange young women smear their faces with lipstick.

Country music and F. Scott Fitzgerald
    On Radio Moscow: "Happy birthday
        To Crystal Gale, indeed let's wish
            A happy birthday to all country stars
                Whose birthdays are today." You need a
        Powerful short-wave radio to escape
    The American cultural drift net. Tony
Was stuck with a dull woman on a cross-Canada train.

I saw them together and took pity,
Sat down with them and chatted for hours.
Next morning, a province along,
My friend complained I was interfering
With his love life. "That wasn't the dull one,
That was a real honey." He looked terribly displeased.
"I've never made love on a train before."

THE GOLDEN TREASURY OF KNOWLEDGE

I

Place the alarm clock far enough from your bed
that you will have to get up to turn it off
but not so far that the sound becomes faint
and you are content to let it ring down
without getting up.

When you do get up to turn off the alarm
let your mind be the centre of flocks of ecstatic birds
and the gently unfolding flowers shivering
with dew in the slanting rays of the rising sun.

Do not under any circumstances return to bed
not even for a few minutes
even if you are certain you won't fall asleep again.

During the first half hour of being up
it is wise to refrain from thinking about your dreams.

II

Agakamunda arundalabatabataba taba
The exact meaning of this phrase is unclear
but it is thought to be an expression of anguish.

One square plus 12 rectangles = 1 window.
With all this light pouring in
where does the darkness go?

Do you talk to God often?
Is His presence clear?

The exact meaning of his presence is unclear
but it is thought to be a tool allowing us
to speak of things we know nothing about.

I saw you get on the bus but I didn't speak
since I felt you did not want to be disturbed.
And when you spoke I saw the bus driver's
eyes fall on mine because he wanted to see
what manner of man such a beautiful radiant
creature was speaking to.
His eyes said Treasure this moment.
You will never drive this route again.
Although I'm sure he had been driving that route
for years.

And then you put your angelic hand on my neck
& your shining head on my chest
& I thought he was going to hit the ditch
in which case he would never have
driven that route again

& others on the bus continued to sit with
frozen suspended inanimate rigid stares
for it was obviously old hat to them
to see a glorious angel wrap her eternal wings
around a grubby weary hopeless wage slave

The light in the light in the light
the nature of which is darkness
& pieces of the sky attached themselves
to branches of dead soot-covered trees
& sprung into life as green leaves
& blossoms swaying in strange breezes
which also made my hair sway
my spine vibrate my fingers ache

my penis erect my ears disappear
my thoughts visible my cells crackle …

I would have gone further but the phone rang.
It was my editor.

III

There are currently 11,000 planes
in the skies over Canada
very few in sight of each other.
If I may be allowed to bare my heart
I'd say I'm aware of my peculiar situation
& the ridiculousness of it but I
continue to exploit it with deadly seriousness
like skilled yogis performing intricate asanas
for howling schoolkids
& I will continue writing this primitive cycle
until the final phone rings

or until I find out why I continue
in which case I will probably continue continuing
like a prisoner in an unlocked cell.
Not that I seriously consider myself primitive
but I'm no impregnable sophisticate like Robbe-Grillet
from whom I've stolen an idea here I think.

What am I talking about? The clock is ticking!
It is the end of another day.
The sky is turning over like a clam.

STORMY JANUARY

I

It is as if I had an eye on the side of my head
just in front of my left ear
and when I turn away from the window
I can still see the falling snow.
The universe is a small place
the size of a booby-trapped toy
(coincidence can kill you). Somehow
it's right that it should snow in January.
No one ever commits suicide during a snowstorm
except for Frank Sinatra in *Young at Heart*.
As I write this I am wearing black socks,
a wine Picasso sweatshirt and blue cords.

Yesterday I met a Jungian scholar who only wanted to talk
about Richard Strauss's influence on Norval Morrisseau.
The man worked as a public relations officer for the ministry
of health and was wearing a Kennedy Space Center T-shirt.
He disagreed when I told him Stanley Kubrick's *2001*
was a remake of Walt Disney's *Fantasia*. Nothing I could
say would make him laugh. I told him my mother was Japanese
but I became disoriented. I spoke of the perfume machine
being out of odour. I spoke of a world of parallel structures,
pigs' ears, mountains with snowy peaks, pyramids, television.
He wasn't even interested when I told him Marjorie had her
hysterectomy on the day Frank and Mona became lovers.

II

When Marjorie got home from the hospital she painted
a picture of herself being struck by lightning.
Months later when Mona became pregnant and Frank

realized his mistake and tried to get back with Marjorie
Marjorie had fallen in love with Jed.

III

Jed had been waiting for Anne to return from Fiji.
Which brings me to my reason for writing.
Anne is expected back from Fiji today.
Canada in January is no place for political
slogans: everything there exists within
a giant spiritual eye as soft as moonlight.
Sometimes I sit in the park and let the snow
pile up around me. The salamander survives the flames
but doesn't necessarily enjoy the experience.
When we are young there are certain people
we know are brighter than we, people who can
exploit their experience in more courageous ways.
When we are older we see we have outlived these people.
They've gone mad and destroyed themselves.

Marx of weakness, marx of woe.
When I turned my head away from the window
I can still see Picasso shrouded in snow.

Sometimes I think I am an eye. At other times, no.

IV

Jim was a painter and a trumpet player, a passionate
drunk who accused everyone of having a Picasso
complex and devised dozens of devious ways
of getting Free Booze. He had grounds privileges
at the psychiatric hospital. One night he was late
returning and was locked out. They found his body
at the foot of the escarpment in the morning.

We wonder at our own lack of courage. We see *High Noon*
and we know we would have joined that posse.
But still we wonder at the urge to survive,
that urge that comes from the flames below,
and I wonder why the angels do not give to others
the same comfort and protection they offer me,
and we wonder at other old friends, successful people
with houses and families, old friends
who do not enjoy anything about their lives,
and we pray to the angels to go to the assistance
of those others but the angels refuse, radiantly.

V

Your political friends will encourage you to forget
the sacredness of the individual baby lamb.
Where the Kootenay and the Columbia rivers finally meet
there is simply silence. I dreamt I was lonely
and I dreamt someone told my mother I wanted
to return to Ontario. The sources of both rivers
are a few miles apart in the Rocky Mountains
but the Kootenay flows north for a thousand miles
and the Columbia south, and when they meet
(just outside my window) there is only silence.
Except for last night when a man, a woman and a baby lamb
appeared (just outside my window). The man
said he'd recently returned from Australia and the woman
said that's a long way from there to here.
She'd just returned from Mexico and he said
did you drink the water? And she said no,
she just drank mescal. It was nice to be home,
thinking of Pablo Picasso again. And they argued
about dams, dams, dams on the Columbia and the Kootenay,
and he said he never saw a dam he didn't like
and she said but dams are ugly and dams damn rivers!
Actually, I quite like McFadden's work.

And the lamb began to speak and said I'd been
in Buddhaland long enough. The Great Cosmic Buddha
wanted you here for some reason and now it wants you
to return, it said. It was as if I had an eye
on the side of my head just in front of my ear.
Everyone was wearing Kennedy Space Center T-shirts that year.
And sometimes I get flashes of the man
I would have been had I been born in another century.
This man is inside me, I can sense him, a happy man,
kind, natural, full of humour and innocence.
He doesn't have hot wires running through his mind
nor does he have steel plates nailed to his flesh.

I can feel his warmth, the rise and fall
of his breath, and his sadness when I manifest
aspects of my severely damaged personality.

But that's enough political sloganeering.

        VI

In the centre of the universe a pair of baby lambs
wrestle in the grass, and there are crocuses,
and bluebells, and drops of dew on every blade,
and there is a cow in the distance, and there is
a plane, a DC-3, flying over the hill.

There's a full moon as we sail into the lagoon
somewhere south of Fiji. Behind us is the forest
thick with snakes and vines and hints of volcanoes.
Random lambs, each shining with a light of its own,
stand on branches of trees. High star-shaped diamonds
hover over our heads. The lambs are staring up at them.
We are full of devotion. Somewhere a woman has just been
told her children have been murdered.
In the centre of the universe is a lamb.

VII

People say to me all the time, they say, Norval
(for that's my name), are you a Jungian?
And I always tell them that when Picasso
died, his spirit entered my body
and there it has remained, and I
don't have to be anything but myself.
And I tell them my mind does not tolerate even its own
systems of thought and experience, nor does it
enjoy its eternal life among the flames
for it is a jealous little mind
that feeds on neo-Platonism in art,
knowledge with which to destroy the minds of others,
and it is anxious for me to die
so that it can enter the minds of others
and destroy them even more completely,
and I'd do anything for it, just anything
and it knows it. Those who can read
can read my autobiography in these paintings,
the story of my flirtations with systematic destruction,
the story of my experiments in trying to discover
how I'd thrive or not in different time frames
with no Third Reich monkey a more or less
permanent resident of my rib cage,
the story of my attempts to track down the lambs
who are said to be wrestling at the centre of the universe,
the story of my attempts to illuminate
in my paintings my own life and the lives
of those who do not want their lives illuminated.

I know I talk a lot but
in a secret ceremony the angels
have made me a priest of light.
The kind of light that is the same as

darkness, a mechanical light,
a night of endless radiance
that animates the universe like the spring
in a little waxwork dummy of Picasso.
My painting is a rocketship to heaven.
My images are cut from the trunks
of living trees. There are no phantoms
in these condensers of memory,
no sense of unattainable reality.
There are no symbols, for as soon
as you decipher the symbols something
dies, an existential integrity.
"To one madness we oppose another."
The most perverse are the innocent
and nature no longer interests even them.
When we are young we are told only the
dull can be content. So we torment
ourselves to demonstrate our intelligence.
We forget to keep our eye on the puck,
your perfect mechanical lamb.

To sum up, only life in the twentieth century
can bring you true peace of mind.

THE ARMADILLO

A woman I hadn't seen in years
phoned today to say she'd come home
and found an armadillo in her kitchen
a live armadillo
quietly eating from the cat's bowl
and it had a collar around its neck
and attached to the collar
was a tag
with my name on it.

What's going on?
she said

and I answered
truthfully
I knew nothing about it.

UNCHAINED MELODY

The house is empty. I'm washing a huge pile of dishes from last night. A bee was sleeping in my handlebars and gave me a sting on my left palm but it only hurt for about four minutes. I'm in love with red-haired Judy Baff two houses south, and dark-haired Pat Petrie in East York. All the doors and windows are open, the happy sun is beaming in, big orange butterflies are having a little strategy session on the porch. Great flapping flocks of Mr. Baff's pigeons are circling the block over and over. I'm singing, screech falsetto, the latest pop song, a painfully slow and emotionally crazed ballad called "Unchained Melody."

When I look up, the kindly old postman is standing like a statue on the verandah glaring through the screen door at me with a look of terrible disappointment on his face. He survived Vimy Ridge and goes to church every Sunday, so I have to pay attention when he gives me that "your generation lacks moral fibre" look. I am very embarrassed and stop singing. He shakes his head and walks away. Once I overheard him telling my father that boys are more "sissified" today than in his time.

It occurs to me I am only singing so loudly (and doing such a photo-finish imitation of the over-the-top lachrymose Roy Hamilton) because the windows are open and maybe Judy Baff will hear me and come tiptoeing over for a matinée performance of the interesting deep soulful kisses we bestowed upon each other in the back row at the Paradox Movie Theatre last Saturday afternoon while Randolph Scott was busy shooting Indians out of trees. This realization does nothing to curb my embarrassment.

I won't be fifteen till the fall and already it's agony being alive.

BATHING IN DIABOLIC ACID

It was a voice on the phone late at night
saying I understand you need a new rear bumper for your car
and later I drove through the rain. And my car
was caked with mud, clumps of weeds
blooming from the tailpipe. And even later
with my beautiful daughters washing their beautiful hair
in a warm house under great heaving thunderstorms
I solemnly wrote a cheque for ten dollars.

These are mediocre moments in a mediocre life
as I bathe daily in diabolic acid.
And I hope I have not bored you
with details of a life you'll never live
being sick enough with your own.
But oh, it ain't so bad. Whenever I'm bored
I bash my forehead against the typewriter
as if it were a perfect little image of the world
as it was on the day I was born.
And somewhere it was raining and someone
was driving to the wrecker's in an old car
covered with mud. Don't wreck that car, I shout.
In 20 years it'll be worth a great deal of money
on the antique market.
                    The moments,
how much more would they be worth?

Further, I have a pair of slippers in my mouth
and a little yellow knife in my heart.
The moments are perplexing me, my lines
have suffered a certain decomposure.
You should have cut it off six lines ago
yet it strikes me as poor form for a poet
to refrain from writing while uninspired.

Anyone can write when inspired. It takes
a master poet to write while uninspired.
Take me for example. When inspired
I have better things to do than compose.
When dull and dry, my normal state,
I write to invoke inspiration
and when it's invoked I quit
and during that gentle swing from A to B
my silly little heart breaks with joy.
Oh, I love it. Oh, I want more and more.
Oh, I never want it to end.

Someday I'll write a big book on prosody
so everyone will be able to avoid writing like me.
It's so difficult. We all talk with the same accent,
we all eat Big Macs. We all agree
poetry is the hard bottom of the lake,
the bed or rock that will never feel the hot
touch of the sun in our lifetime. It would
have been a mysterious death. It will always be
a mysterious life, plenty of rocks
to sun on in sunny Ontario or Quebec.

A CUP OF TEA WITH ISSA

I've never seen a raindrop fall on a frog's head but you have. You say the frog wiped away the water with his wrist and that's good enough for me.

Ever since I first heard it fifteen years ago your poem on the death of your son has been flitting in and out of my mind. And now I see there are two versions, the first having been revised on the later death of your daughter, in 1819, of smallpox. And now I want you to know that I hope you've been reunited with your sons and your daughters and your wives and your father, and that I prefer the first version.

The sun has dropped behind the mountains and the tiny cars on the long winding road way over on the other side of the lake have their lights on. And a sense of amazement springs up, amazement that we live in a world where the sun continually rises and sets.

The *Marasmius oreades* (delicious when fried with bacon) have formed a fairy ring in the shape of a giant number 3 in the courtyard lawn, reminding me of the time I saw three motorcycles parked diagonally at the curb in front of 111 Brucedale Avenue.

In October you can look at the sides of the mountains and see the patterns made by the deciduous trees which have become bright yellow or orange among the coniferous which have remained dark green. Sometimes it seems like a territorial war up there but the conflict between the two types of trees is probably more in my mind than on the slopes.

This morning the sky is blue but the tops of the mountains cling to thick giant puffs of pink and grey cloud. A small white cloud rises from the surface of the lake and tries to reach the big ones up above but by the time it gets halfway there it has almost completely disappeared.

It's pleasant to be so unhurried that you can see even the slowest-moving clouds moving. A part of me says I should be ashamed of myself but you know the more time you waste the more you get. It's like money.

On a rainy windy October morning a grey Volkswagen sits at the side of the road. It's covered with hundreds of small wet yellow leaves plastered on the trunk, on the hood, on the roof — in a strangely satisfying pattern. Was it the rain and the wind or was it a subtle and patient artist with a pot of glue? Of course it was the wind and the rain and of course it's a hackneyed idea. But for a moment I wonder. As you would have.

It's pleasant to have a cup of tea and think of you, Issa, and to think of others in the twentieth century having a cup of tea and thinking of you, Issa.

THE SEDUCTION OF QUEEN ELIZABETH II

What a day this has been! I don't have any legs and I just finished seducing Queen Elizabeth II! It was about four months ago that I first decided to seduce the Queen. Some jealous fanatic heard about my plans and shot off my legs. I'm still not recovered but when I woke up this morning I just knew today was the day. I dreamt I was being chased by an army of ants. When I looked close each ant was goose-stepping and had a little Hitler moustache. Just like the old philosopher in the death camp, I dived into the latrine — the one place they wouldn't follow me.

I woke up and noted the pain in my stumps had decreased. It usually does after I dream about ants. So I knew this was the day. For practise I went over to my parents' place and seduced my mom and dad. I sent my dad to the store for some beer and while he was gone I seduced my mom. Then when my mom was in the garden picking me a bouquet of forget-me-nots I seduced my dad. Boy, did he love it! Then I went home and sent my wife over to the welfare office to see about my new motorized wheelchair. While she was gone I seduced my children, all of them, two boys and two girls ages nine to fifteen. Boy, were they surprised!

Then I nipped over to Buckingham Palace and seduced the Queen. It was really quite easy. I wheeled in backwards so it looked as if I were leaving. I wheeled right up to the Queen's rooms and there she was counting her money. I told her I knew something that was even more fun than counting your money. "Oh?" she said, her nostrils all aquiver. "And what would that be, pray tell?" Next thing she knew we were in the royal sack. Maybe I didn't have any legs but I could still stand at attention. Imagine me, Davy Macfadgen, in bed with the Queen! It didn't last long though for after a few minutes my stumps started to hurt and I had to withdraw. She was obviously terribly disappointed to see me go but, as befits a Queen, she didn't ask when she could see me again. Not sure I'd want to anyway. I mean some things you really only need to do once, right?

And how would I rate the Queen in bed? Superior. Best I've had in fact. Worth losing your legs over? That's a tough question. It's true I'll never walk again like an ordinary person. And yet I'll always have the memory of having had the best in bed.

TIBETAN MONOLOGUE

When you're driving along a winding mountain road
during a blizzard
and a transport truck passes you
splattering slush all over your windshield
and causing you to go out of control
and roll over in the ditch
the driver of the truck
was your father in a previous incarnation.

When you're getting loaded
in a sleazy bar on Davie Street
and a fourteen-year-old in spike boots
and a pink mohair sweater
asks you if you want a blow job
and you ask how much
and she says two bucks
that girl
was your mother in a previous incarnation.

When you're flying over British Columbia
in a Pacific Western Boeing 747
and you've got a head cold and your
eustachian tubes are all plugged up
and the pressure is getting more and more intense
and soon you're holding your head in agony
even screaming
and your eardrums are forming bubbles
like thin membranes of bubblegum
and your eyes are bulging
like Halloween candy apples
with razor blades in them
and you're just going crazy for the plane to land
and the pilot announces that the plane won't be landing

at Castlegar
because of fog conditions
it will have to go on to Cranbrook
and an hour later the pilot announces
they can't land at Cranbrook either
and they're going to turn around and fly back
to Vancouver
and see if they might be able to land there
and you're screaming for help
and everyone is ignoring you
because there's nothing they can do anyway
everybody was your mom and dad
in previous incarnations.

SECRETS OF THE UNIVERSE

You're waiting for a bus at Ward and Baker
and a woman comes up to you
and asks for a dance.

You tell her you don't want to dance
for there is too much snow
and not enough music
and she says you didn't mind
dancing with me last night.

And when you tell her she's mistaken
you didn't dance with her or anyone last night
she says oh yes you did
and when you ask where
she says up there
on the roof
and she points to the roof of Hipperson Hardware.

In fact, she says, as her voice drops
and a shy look comes into her eyes
I've even danced with you on other planets
Venus and Mars for instance
and then she walks away

leaving you to wonder about the part of your life
that is secret even from you.

ANTICIPATING A TRIP TO ONTARIO

Wearing a watch that once belonged
to Robert Louis Stevenson
the famous actor David Niven
sat at the kitchen table questioning my wisdom
in having pictures of you on the wall.
We'd been eating cream cheese and tomato sandwiches.
A full moon was setting behind the Kokanee Glacier
like a blob of butter dissolving in hot tea.
Suddenly he coughed and slumped in his chair
and his wife said my God he's had a heart attack,
and then he vanished in a puff of invisible smoke.
I looked all around the room, even under the table.
Eerie pounding noises started coming from the walls.
I looked at the cream cheese on the table.
The expiry date was on the wrapper: June 7.
By then, I thought, I'll be in Ontario.

MEANINGLESS MIDNIGHT MUSINGS

I have so much to write & nothing to write about,
writing far into the night when I should be spending time
with real people with ugly fat & hairy ears
instead of the perfect gods & goddesses
I imagine reading this & nodding
Yes, through him I see my own greatness....

I'm no ant. I'm not trying to build a perfect society.
I'm all gross rotting imperfections of selfishness, I'm
interested in my own personal world.

I'm addicted to toothpicks.

I've got no orderliness in my life. I look
in others' faces to see if their blackheads
are as ugly as mine, into their eyes
to see my blockhead's reflection.

I'll soon be out of this depression.
At least I'm not holding my wife & kids at bay
with a double-barrelled shotgun, that would be
depression.

Diary of a pig. Even a pig is born & dies.
Even a pig is ignorant. Why must I be different?

I am burning with a pure, pure light.

I want a colour TV. A new car.
I want to be a whale in the Indian Ocean.
I want everyone to have fun.

What should I wear?
Should I have my torn trousers mended?
Why do I like corduroy so much?
Why do people like me so much?

Judge Walter Tuchtie: "What were you doing
in the Wentworth House? Why weren't you at home
with your wife & four kids?"

Here comes my wife, hope she doesn't see this.

I used to ride downtown every day with Ray,
in Ray's car. He's a foreman in a body shop,
Mercanti Auto Body. He gets a new car every year
supplied by the company.
He always stops at Tim Hortons for donuts.
He always talks knowledgeably about the weather.
He knows all about birds & animals & the winds.
His wife is having awful problems with her face,
painful operations, skin grafts.
It all started with a fall.

I hope nothing like that ever happens to my wife.

Sometimes I used to drive downtown with Muriel.
She has an old white rusty Chev. She's always
about to get a new one but never does. Then
she's always going to move out on her parents
but she never does. She works in
the VD clinic. She gets a lot of inside dope.
Now I leave later in the morning. And it's April,
spring you know.

            I like to stroll to the bus stop,
about half a mile. I like the people who take the bus.

I often sit next to Mrs. Lachance. She has a fat ass,
I don't think she'd mind me telling you. She gets off
one stop before me. She gets on the bus first
then stands beside the seat she wants to sit down on
then says to me: "Are you going to sit with me?"
in a nice sweet schoolgirl's voice. & I say
I guess so. So I squeeze past her & sit down
then she comes in behind me,
                                        real secure I feel.
Bus can bounce all it wants I won't move.
She's from Prince Edward Island. She left home at 17,
came to Ontario, her sister went to California.
It's cheaper to phone from California to Ontario
than the other way around. That burns my ass she says.

Once when Allen Ginsberg was here last summer she was seen
flying out of her house & running over to the neighbour's
screaming Allen Ginsberg just went into the McFaddens'!!!
She keeps an eye on me. She works as a teller
in the bank where I have my so-called account.

To be truthful I am getting sick of trying to write
beauty in poems....
Life is not that kind of beautiful, that sense of
attempting to find a moment's beauty no longer exists.
There are no special moments.

Well yes, there are special moments but they are not
special. I mean what is special? Wally Zimmerman
is the special narcotics prosecutor. Is there
something special about this poem? Does it remind you
of Wally Zimmerman?

I want to re-read everything of Thomas Hardy's. Like a
madman with a rope I want to hang everything.

I'm riddled with insanity, neither sane nor saintly.

Red-haired laughing Kelly Smith I love you & I'm sorry
if I hurt you. He pleaded guilty to breaking into
Mrs. Smith's house & making lunch for himself two days in a row,
Mrs. Smith coming home from work finding the kitchen a mess,
food all over, fridge door agape.
So he got nine months. I asked the cop if the kid
was any relation to Mrs. Smith. Cop said no, just
a coincidence.
                    So I wrote the story, it appeared
on page 8: Smith & Mrs. Smith are not related.

Later I find out Mrs. Smith is Kelly Smith's mother no less
& he's upset by the news story, thinks she's disowned him.
The back door was open, he says; he was hungry.
He did borrow his brother's coat & boots
but he didn't steal that necklace & diamond ring.

I'm sorry I said that about no relation, that's what
the cop told me.
                    Didn't bother me, he said.

If for one month I could fly that would be a
special month.
What would people say if I could fly?
Would it put a strain on my marriage?
Would my wife still love me?
Would she insist I teach her to fly
even if I lacked the power to pass on my knowledge?
What would Lloyd Abbey say? Would he be jealous?
Or would he decide to forgive me for my sins?
Would it disrupt the whole city to see me flying
to work in the morning, happy, soaring gaily?
Would people notice or would they merely shrug?

Would they get used to it after a couple of days?
Would kids be bored to see me running down the
street then lifting up my legs & taking off?

I wonder if it's cold up there. Would you have to wear
a special suit even in summer? If so I'd just fly low,
skimming over the trees. Ah! soon the trees will be green!

I told Victor Coleman about certain flying fantasies I had.
Oh how I wish I hadn't told! He sneered
& said "Repressed sexuality!" Oh!

Like a lightning silver suppository I clip through
the green & pink atmosphere of earth
like a bus cuts a corner, one wheel going up on the curb,
people stepping back to save toes.

We'll have to do something to curb taxes!

Poems that go on into the night like short-wave stations.
Strangely illuminated occurrences waiting forever for remembrance.

Black & white pussy cat at cellar window
doesn't look in, just sidles by not wondering
if anyone's down there.

The moon is round. The earth is round.
Everything is round, round, round, round.

The moon doesn't exist but it has all the properties
of something that actually exists.

The moon is a nearby planet, a star, a cold sun.
The sun is much further away than the moon.
The moon is jealous of comets. Even the sun
is considering registering an official complaint.

The sun & the moon & of course the more distant
planets & stars would be amazed if they knew
that the earth has a thin layer of people.
Each human being is as intelligent as the moon.
The earth itself is no smarter than one single person.
The individual person is very small so to speak
but he knows everything!

The moon goes around & around the earth never dreaming
that billions of pairs of eyes are on it.

All the planets & that are copies of each other.
The electrical core of no-space leaked out & created
planets, suns, the spatial heavens, celestial glory.
Then the electrical cores of planets leaked out
& human life evolved.

A poem is a hex to prevent repetition.
Freedom from the cycle of birth & rebirth.
Her blouse was all undone. Her breasts
smelled like butter.

My eyes went inside my head. One got caught
in my eardrum. The other I swallowed.

I'm glad that April's here. The bus won't
be getting bombarded by snowballs all the time.
Those dumb kids are going to hurt somebody.

HOW TO BECOME PART OF NATURE

Pay your bills promptly
Keep track of everything you spend
Take taxis everywhere you go
Avoid people you're naturally attracted to
Discuss the weather with strangers
Make random phone calls at 2 a.m.
Neither apologize nor forgive
Avoid curiosity
Always wear blue suits
Never smile
Tell long boring stories
Yawn when people are talking to you
Avoid sex whenever possible
Complain loudly about unions
Cultivate a British accent
Make obscene gestures at nuns
Never fart in public
Rattle change in your pocket
Flush newspapers down public toilets
Lecture people about smoking
Collect pornography
Be the first to pass out at parties
Debunk current fads
Keep your eyes unfocussed

This is all you need to know. Within three years
of following these rules carefully
you will be part of nature.

DEAD HIPPOPOTAMUS

You're right: my poems are seldom as quiet as they could be. I want them
flower-like and full of equilibrium, their power deeply buried. Quietly
reflecting the quiet and unregarded miracles occurring all around them.
They should never worry about being noticed among all the other poems.
If they are truly and sincerely blossom-like and in addition technically well
constructed it would be impossible for them to envy the poems of others.
And so I slept poorly after our visit last night and in the morning I went out
for a paper and coffee and there at the corner of Parliament and Carlton
was a dead hippopotamus. It had been in a collision with two cars and was
lying there, its eyes already sunken and dry with death, its thick flesh
dull and dusty. It looked stupid lying there, a beast never to roam again.
In a land in which such beasts are not native, are kept locked up in zoos,
it reminded me of the long-delayed death of exotic but ridiculous dreams.

When I was a cowboy in Alberta we once found a calf wandering half-starved
and it was obvious the mother had died. And so we rode out looking for her.
She'd crawled into a small wooden shed and died there and in the summer heat
her carcass had bloated until it filled the entire shed and it kept bloating
until the shed had slowly exploded from the internal pressure. And the horrid
flyblown stench under the blue sky and white clouds of the endless prairie,
far from roads. Like these grossly bloated sonnets, bursting through the
shed of common poetic decency. As for the hippo, there was no stench,
no bloating, just a dry rot from within, a terrible dryness and lack of life.
And it looked as if it had been dead centuries, drowned in an African bog,
then discovered and placed at a busy intersection to advertise traffic safety.
Well, the things you said last night, there is nothing I want to do. We had
the occasional taste of bliss together over the years and my or was it our
fantasy that someday we'd be free to live together and experience that bliss
constantly was the psychological equivalent of a big stupid hippo covered
with birds and flies and drinking swamp water tainted with assorted poisons.
"I think I need your poems more than your poems need me, and I'm not just
saying that to be polite," you said. But you also said you found them often
too attentive, too clever, and they tended to dominate you in a way that was

sometimes exhausting, sometimes frightening, sometimes demonic. Your criticism
I accept easily, in fact I probably knew all along the poems were all wrong,
they tried to accomplish certain things, they even tried to manipulate your
emotions, they flexed their biceps on beaches, they posed in front of mirrors,
they were irresponsible, tried to tell you things that perhaps were not true.
This represents another in a long line of betrayals of the spirit of poetry.
Poems are not meant to persuade, exhaust, frighten, they are not meant to
say what cannot be said with a quiet glance, and one should not write so
many of them that they are in danger of being in collision with dumb animals.

THE WOUND

The beautiful young woman was severely injured.
I carried her off the road & placed her
on the grassy bank of a clear deep cold stream.
I put her legs in the water & lowered her jeans.
She had a deep wound across her lower abdomen.
I gently pushed her entrails back into the wound.
Three doctors floated downstream on a raft.
They smiled knowingly & complimented me on my first aid.
They took the woman away with them on the raft.

AN UNEXPECTED CHEQUE FOR $86

October 21, 1969

                    An unex-
            pected cheque for $86
                    arrived in the mail
on the day Jack Kerouac died
& a cold wind toppled
            garbage cans & confused
                    birds
as I walked over to the bank
a little sick in my stomach
with my favourite writer &
            all-time hero
safe in heaven at last
& looking down on me & every-
                                body
with never-ending interest
on our long lonely walks
            towards the bank.

THIN GYPSY WOMAN

*An anorexic Gypsy sleeps over. As she sleeps the poet writes, revealing rather
unpleasant aspects of his character. After "Una Strana Zingarella" by Dino
Campana (1885-1932).*

Here comes my poem, slipping coolly
Through the mossy quiet of my room
While your head turns on its pale pillow
And you continue inhaling all the
Vapours of your magnetic dreams.
The moon's tuckered out and snoring.
The olive trees are silent. A drunkard
Somewhere sings himself to sleep.

You have stayed, thin Gypsy woman,
Lonely and with such lovely hair,
Thin horizontal scars running up
Each arm like ladders of despair.
Listen to my poem in the cool night air,
I want to see your split ends dancing
Bonily on your yellow shoulders.
So turn to me and listen to my poem.

You've no smell! You're pure as sound!
Yikes! You smile when you kiss me
But your kisses are bitter and full of sorrow.
Your lovely eye sparkles too much,
It has a doomed look about it.
If I can persuade you to sing for me
Your voice will be blade-sharp as a violin
Played in a small room at three in the morning.

Would you accept this bottle of Shalimar?
Why do you go out dressed in blood?
Do you like to visit old country churches?

Of course you're afraid of perfume:
Your body's too thin, your eyes too dark.
But I'd love to see your soul tremble,
And your eyes grow big and round.

Also your sweetly anaemic saint
(Whom you had to try to seduce
As he knelt and spread his clouds of incense),
Praising Christ with all his passion —
And with nothing left for you.
Christus vicisti:
The ivory of your crucifix
Is a purer white than your belly's.
You are not as sweet and glorious,
Dark wrinkles like crows tremble
Among the vertiginous grey shadows.

And you would kneel and weep, your hands
Covering your eyes, your long thin feet
Solid on the earth like the feet
Of an unnameable and untameable beast.
What would your tiny tears taste like?
Maybe a bit like flames?

At the hour of my death I would like to be
Wearing a fantastic diadem composed
Of such terrible tears, this would allow
The little demons with cloven hooves
To take me into their deepest confidence.
Oh, how could I be saying such things
To you, my solemn friend?
It's the tragic spell woven by

Your lovely hair perhaps, or else because
You dress in red and have no smell.

POP

I open the door & walk in
& little Alison comes running towards me
she has a limp yellow balloon in her hand
& asks me to inflate it, Daddy

It's almost bedtime & she
is wearing her pink nightgown
candy-striped white & pink

& the balloon has printed on itself
in neat little type
FIGHT CYSTIC FIBROSIS
GIVE A CHILD THE BREATH OF LIFE

I blow the balloon up & the type
increases in size about 10 times
(grows quickly from little to large)
(grows like magic)

(it would be nice if books
came in adjustable type
& nice if I could blow myself up
into John Keats' size

I've been reading John Keats

one day John coughed onto his sleeve
a little blood, he was 26
& knew death was nigh
[149 years ago this month]
so he wrote a letter to each of his friends
saying I'm going to die now)

I tell Alison to keep the balloon
away from the cat & she says why?
& I say 'cause the cat'll break it
& you will cry

A little later I hear from the kitchen
that characteristic POP of a burst balloon
followed by no crying.

AN INVENTORY OF MY POSSESSIONS

A few ideas not worth listing.

A desire for unblemished serenity.

A strange lack of desire for romance.

A sad feeling because I would give up everything for you but you would
give up nothing for me.

A window looking west along Phipps and a window looking north along
Saint Nicholas.

A swirl of memories that follow me around like hungry cocker spaniels.

A pair of bookshelves designed and built by Robert Fones thirteen years
ago.

A PowerBook 170 bought at Elm Street Computer from Sam Schwartz,
Super Salesman.

A PLW300 printer bought at the same place, with a *huge* discount for
promising to mention Sam in this poem.

An old scanner donated by Stan Bevington.

A sadly incomplete collection of everything published by Coach House
Press in happier days.

A nostalgia for the days before Stan Bevington bought his first Porsche.

A set of Hamilton Tiger-Cat beer glasses, a set of Col. John McCrae
(author of "In Flanders Fields") Branch 234 Royal Canadian Legion
Grand Opening Sept. 10/77 beer glasses, a souvenir bottle of Thomas
Hardy's Ale and a small china bust of Mozart.

A sick feeling about living in a country with no national culture next to a
country that has a huge national culture that is spiritless, heartless,
vulgar and excessively profit-driven.

A strange case of time-and-space claustrophobia.

A television that gets no channels and a VCR that plays Pedro Almodóvar
and Luis Buñuel movies over and over.

Two Spanish-language teachers (Carmen from Madrid and María Dolores
from Murcía) who don't know of each other's existence.

An electric fan for the summer and an electric heater for the winter.

Three boom boxes, one short-wave radio and three pairs of headphones
made in Ireland.

Two compact-disc players.

A faded old Curious George stuffed monkey hanging by its left heel from the ceiling in front of the west window with a big smile on his face.

John B. Boyle's "Spanish Heel" hanging from the ceiling.

Seja Stevenson's giant brightly coloured stuffed "M" hanging from the ceiling.

A trumpet once used by Sir Charles G. D. Roberts hanging from the ceiling by its second valve.

My father's World War II dog tags hanging from the ceiling by their original string.

Two lamps and no lava.

A Boston Self-Feeder donated by my father in 1959.

A Waterman fountain pen that writes like a dream.

A bed (that has seen better nights).

Two chairs.

Two desks, including a beautiful old oak desk purchased privately from Isaac Abrahamson in Hamilton, Ontario, on Oct. 11, 1977.

An electric kettle.

A feeling of excitement because Niagara peach season is just around the corner.

The complete works of Manuel de Falla, Bob Marley, the Acid Junkies, De Dannan and Holly Cole on compact disc.

The complete works of Vladimir Nabokov, Robertson Davies, Carlos Castaneda, William Shakespeare and Charles Dickens in book form.

A huge pile of books each of which I want to read immediately, and with luxurious slowness.

A large canvas Canada Post mailbag full of laundry.

A letter from Sheila Curnoe.

A strange curiosity to know at any moment of the day or night what Dany Laferrière is doing.

A box of old family photos going back to 1880.

A penchant for causing trouble without meaning to.

Euphoria on account of the advent of the long-anticipated abatement of passions and appetites that takes place after the half-century mark.

Euphoria at the deaths of some of my friends who were far too good for this garbage dump of a world.

A desire to outlive my father but not my daughters.

A great certainty that my death will leave you largely unmoved, which bothers me not at all, really.

A blue suit made in Hamilton by my old childhood friend Teddy the Tailor.

A grey double-breasted suit made in Germany and sold to me dirt cheap by a Trinidadian tailor on Yonge Street who was going out of business on account of failing eyesight (my envious neighbour Michael Coren refers to this as my "pimp suit" because it only has one button).

A lightweight black suit for travelling to non-English-speaking countries.

A genuine Blue Jays cap.

A rather handsome Stetson porkpie hat made out of coconut fibre.

A Maple Leafs toque.

A Donegal tweed motoring cap that fits like a dream.

A pair of brown Boulet cowboy boots.

Three pairs of Rockports, including one pair donated by Ian McConnell.

A pair of Sunday-best burgundy Bostonians that look like a million but only cost a hundred bucks in a store on Bloor Street hard-hit by the recession.

A modest collection of original Kureleks, Kiyookas, Curnoes, Dewdneys and Boyles on the wall.

A copy of *Don Quixote* owned by my mother as a child and rubber-stamped with her name.

The complete Upanishads in four volumes translated by Swami Nikhilananda.

A diary kept by my grandfather George Brown McFadden during World War II.

A Bible filled with doodles executed by my Welsh grandfather John Pidgeon during his childhood years at Blue School, Wells, also a gold chain presented to him for being the national chairman of the International Order of Odd Fellows Manchester Unity in 1908 at the age of twenty-one.

A pair of black oxfords donated by Sandy Segal's boyfriend.

Three framed photos of me and my brother as kids, one of which won Dad first prize (eleven dollars) in a photo contest sponsored by *Stelco Flashes* in 1954.

A slide projector and sixteen boxed carousels of slides from the major galleries of the world.

One house plant.

One ostrich feather.

Two Spanish skin mags and a pair of Celestron Ultima 10x50 field glasses.

A dozen pairs of green silk boxer shorts.

A very long and heavy Donegal tweed topcoat for cold Toronto winters.

A 1964 *Encyclopaedia Britannica* donated by Cathie Forgie.

A sarcastic tongue, but only when riled.

A low centre of gravity, a Taoist-like gait and a habit of breathing slowly.

Several former girlfriends who still love me more than you ever will, which isn't saying much.

A love of my neighbourhood but a dislike of Toronto in general.

A chequing account and a credit card.

Muddled memories of many previous lives.

Two doctors, one accountant, no lawyers.

Tons of good luck, and an understanding that it could change at any time, with no warning.

A modest collection of old postcards showing tinted photographic scenes from Southern Ontario in the twenties and thirties.

Three cameras, most notably a Nikon F3 with two lenses, a 35mm and a 105.

A fifty-five gallon drum of solid dimethyltryptamine.

A number of regrets, softened (conveniently) by my belief in the illusory nature of pain, free will, individuality, time, space, consciousness and existence.

A beautiful new limited-edition book called *Waiting for Alice* by Victor Coleman, with original watercolours by Mike Hansen, and, to pay for the book, a postdated cheque made out to Victor in the amount of $125 which I am about to post to him, two weeks late, along with a copy of this poem.

Toronto, Ontario
June 10/95
(postdated)

AN HOUR'S RESTLESS SLEEP

1

An hour's restless sleep
and I'm awake
shaken awake by the real
enormity of the crime

feeling the last warmth evaporate
from the body of the Rev. Martin Luther King,
holy man of man, son of man.

Nothing can compare with such a crime.
The destruction of a man full of the radiance of peace,
unashamed, shining forth his divinity and perfect human loveliness,
the embodiment of what when I was a kid I thought that's what it is to be a
    man
and I now see never, it will never be like that to be a man —
a million years from now, if the race still be alive
it will still on occasion give birth to such perfection
and such perfection will again be murdered
in his 33rd or 39th year.

2

Oh God, are you happy? One little bullet in the neck and he would stay
    alive for an hour, unable to speak, knowing —
the radiant one full of love at his own eternally repeated death,
for there is no hate can come from the son of man, like in some people you
    can burn a rotten log and have the bugs come out
but here we have no bugs, no rot,
all can come out is purity and love and peace and yearning to see my
    brother radiant, in his own way.

"O The Martyr's sigh is the angel's Sword," said William Blake
and I'm not sure I know what that means and it's not at all comforting ...

3

This world known as Earth, Earth of journalism and common sense,
covered with fresh waters and oceans and fish, and mountains and forests,
    prairies
and a sun to go round and round it continuously without the slightest
    variation or complaint, endlessly shining —
it has produced a strange race for its own mirror, and this race has strange
    eccentric passions that are completely divorced from the business of
    sweet life and death,
the passion of see how poor you can keep your brother, see how mean he
    can get
and finally, hey man I need something long and hard to shoot people with,
    for the one nature provided is all full of constrictions oh Jesus Christ....

4

If I waited a few days I could make a well-wrought poem out of this, but
    hell this is my way.
And I could say:
Hey some are born with hearts of love, hearts functioning well, as the sixth
    sense
and some are born with hearts of ignorance, lumps of coal scratching
    together,
for the heart in its proper usage is a better sense than ear or eye and a better
    tool than trigonometry.
But if you're born with a heart that works well, and you find it natural that
    your heart be your sixth sense
(and as I write this the wind howls around television aerials and windows
    rattle, and my wife cries oh everything's all wrong with the world),
well if you got that, you keep quiet about it, try to enjoy it or enter a
    monastery that specializes in collecting dimes for Africa or something

because Martin Luther King was much more than a man with a good heart —
he was the radiance of the ages and the sun and moon and stars, yea the
        whole solar system was inside him and he tried ...
and what good did he do? eh? what good did he do, friend, did he do any
        good, what is there he left changed for the better?
Not a thing, all he got was fame. And fatherless children, husbandless wife. A
        name to remember with derision. A bullet in the neck. A bad example.

5

Oh the blood has stopped flowing, the body's warmth has flown away, the
        poem has stopped flowing, but still, all over the world, the tears continue
        flowing,
thinking, for instance, of the last hour of peaceful agony of this man of man
the thoughts passing through his speechless mind, did he think of Eliot's
        prophetic irony "April is the cruellest month"?
or of his wife whom he wouldn't see in old age, children he wouldn't see in
        maturity, bombs he wouldn't see stop falling falling falling in his beloved
        Asia
and the agony of not knowing the effectiveness of his long sacrifice, or of the
        realization of its total vanity or what?
and the big animal existence of the man so perfectly balanced and fading away
        of an early Thursday evening early April Tennessee
and the news spreading around the world electronically ...

6

So I say unto all whose hearts know what I'm saying, know about dreams and
        visions so cruelly implanted, of brotherhood and peace and freedom from
        hunger and poverty if you have a heart that knows what I say,
then become a poet at the most. Write little poems about it, because this race
        collects poems for all time, without understanding them, and in case of
        any remarkable change in the human direction, your poems may be
        someday meaningful.

Or get up there and be like King, and sacrifice your animal existence and
    vegetative delights and family love relations of adoration,
because this race also collects stories of assassinations, crucifixions and
    martyrdoms, whatever, for whatever surface meaning,
and someday, three or four thousand years from now your superhuman
    efforts and perfect human heart may take on some meaning.

7

I change that now,
I know he did good stuff, his life wasn't meaningless.
He had the spirit of Walt Whitman in his right hand
and the spirit of William Blake in his left
and the spirit of John the Baptist in his forehead.

If at any time a dove had landed on his head I would not have thought
    anything of it.
He got the Civil Rights Law passed in his own home area, Southern U.S.A.
    — law that says
you can't pick and choose who gets on the bus or stays at your inn —
you gotta take 'em as they come
(as I write I can hear King's voice reading this out loud in my head, or is he
    dictating?) (King's voice is a bit different now that he no longer feels
    the need for a composed personality, he's a bit looser on the surface ...)

Yes, King put a lot of hope into people's hearts momentarily and now he's
    dead at thirty-nine and now the bloody war comes, the one Christ
    couldn't prevent, perhaps wouldn't want to,
and someday after everyone who was contemporary with King is dead
the social structure of the world will be altered into such a pattern
that anyone who wants to grow up and be a holy man of God, or wants to
    be a man of love and peace, well he can,
he can walk the earth with his heart as big or small as he wants it
and King will be remembered as the man who showed the war had to be

and somehow, every man, woman and child who ever drew breath will be
    remembered
and will walk in glory forever.

8

Martin Luther King is up in heaven now.
Up there waiting to meet him were all the other great Americans who ever
    lived: Walt Whitman.
King shook Walt's hand then excused himself,
went off to be alone with his thoughts for a billion years.

9

Oh sorrow so deep, shot through and through with sorrow,
as though this murder was enacted on a deeper and truer plane than the
    plane on which we live from day to day,
as though this murder is something enacted deep inside every man's life at
    one time only,
as if this murder snapped the membrane that separated my personal
    energies from the primal energies of the universe,
as if this murder snapped the membrane that separated my sorrow from my
    joy,
so that from this day until my death I'll be a man conscious of the universal
    texture of my life,
a man who carries around inside himself the death of all things like an
    eternally flowering vine,
blessed forever, for the eternally flowering vine is the eternally blessed
    universal man
who is born and dies endlessly, complete with the total history of life and
    the total future of life,
in the form of a sense of everything that has happened and everything that
    will ever happen,
and I'll sing till the day I die, for in the flesh I'm face to face with the most
    awful horrors and the greatest perfections of life,

and in the flesh I'm face to face with Martin Luther King, Walt Whitman,
   William Blake, John the Baptist, Jesus Christ and all the Buddhas
   stretching in long unknown lines into the past and future,
and in my sorrow I'm full of endless music and endless discovery stretching
   in long unknown lines into past and future, concentrically from my
   radiant centre, at the horrible murder of the Rev. Martin Luther King,
   holy man of man, son of man.

A JEWEL BOX

The little girl was 10.
I fancy she said
"I'm 10 and drowning"
as the lake folded over her
layer upon layer, wave
upon wave, sun upon
sun, perfectly,
separating her from things,
squeezing out her connections,
swallowing her power.

Maybe her brain's last picture
was of her jewellery box.
I hold it in my hands, now, with fear.
It's the girl's drowned head:
painfully handcarved, lost.
Mocking human love. And
something of the dead girl
comes up inside me
moving me with love
to love that jewelled box.

AFTER THOMAS HARDY'S "AFTERWARDS"

After I'm dead
& time
continues on without me
much as it did before I was born

a child will pick up
a piece of dog shit
& taste it

& someone will say Look!
McFadden was a man who
would have noticed that.

A JAR OF BUTTERFLIES

Brian Jones of the Rolling Stones
died the other day at 26
& two days later the Stones
had a big free concert at Hyde Park
an audience of thousands,
a packed park
              & a jar of butterflies
was let loose in Brian's memory.

              I wasn't there
              so why write about it?

They're all going to die, everyone
in that audience of thousands
& all the butterflies & even
this whole planet & solar system.

The whole human race is going to die
& I'll be dead before you know it
& I won't cry for me
if you don't cry for you.

It'll take a million years for the planet
to backtrack to where it was
before the human race was isolated
& even then it'll be that much older
& closer to its own death
death by falling into the sun
death by the sun going cold.

All around us are other planets
of intelligence experimenting
with intelligent forms of life.

Nature is a spirit so intelligent
because it's absorbed in the past
so many intelligent but extinct
forms of life
              & man'll go back
back into that formless spirit
one, like a harmonious community
joyful with scientific contemplation.

THE RAT

I am taking care of Virginia
while her mother attends summer school
and over the radio comes the news
that deadly disease-carrying rats
have invaded the lower Muskokas.

Then a rat
with a human-looking face
darts past the cottage
and I turn to see Virginia
writhing on the ground.

I look again and she's dead.

I take off with a knife.
I hope to catch the rat and kill it
before it kills others.

It runs into a crowded store
and I manage to corner it
and pounce on it
and I hold its teeth away from my arms
by pressing the knife against its neck
and as I hesitate
the rat turns into a young girl
about Virginia's age
extremely frightened.

I begin hacking at her neck
until long streams of blood begin spurting
and soon she is dead

and when I look up
dozens of people are staring at me
with horrified faces.

To them I've just murdered
an innocent child.

THE ESKIMO WHO LACKED PERFECTION

My grandmother was Portuguese or Egyptian or something
said Chuck Arcadie of Inuvik explaining why he has curly hair
rare for an Eskimo, and explaining why his right arm and leg
seemed kind of stiff, he said he fell ten feet from a schooner
onto a steel barge at Aklavik when he was seven,
landing on his head. I've been a cripple ever since,
he said. I wish I was more perfect. But every year
I think I get better and better.

                                 Someone told me
Chuck was a poet so I asked for some poems.
He recited several good ones from memory, including a long one
called "Complicated Masterpiece," and it really was.
He said every new love affair brings more poems in its wake.
With his curly hair, large dark eyes, and lameness
he reminded me of Lord Byron, so I told him, but Chuck
knew as much about Byron as Byron knew about him.
And so I told him Byron was a nineteenth-century English poet
who had considerable success with women,
and Chuck got excited and said, Really? Can you
jot down his name for me? Are there any books about him?

And Chuck told me about the Golden Gloves trophy
he won, lightweight category, and the territorial championship
he won two years running, or rather boxing —
And I told him he couldn't be that much of a cripple
if he was such a good boxer
but he said he trained really hard
to compensate for his lameness
and he could have been a famous athlete
if it hadn't been for that fall.

He said he was aware of all his imperfections
and he described himself and I quote as a bastard,
lame, curly-haired Eskimo born about 1946
somewhere near Tuktoyaktuk
and he wanted to find a woman whose mind
would inspire him to greatness.

He said trapping was the only life
but being a cripple he couldn't trap.
He was working for Canada Manpower
and thinking of going to university.
He told me all you need is faith
and you can do anything you want.
Then he asked me what I would do
if I were him. And close to suffocating
with the horror of being white
and of being responsible for his pain
all I could say was how would you
answer that question if you were me?

And he said he's glad the white man came
for he would have been allowed to die, being lame,
forgetting it was the white man's steel barge
that crunched his brain.

Some greedy entrepreneurs from up south
were walking down the hot and dusty boardwalk
of Mackenzie Street in suits and vests and ten-dollar ties
with briefcases full of unsigned contracts
and I asked Chuck why he figured
they were dressed like that in all that heat

and he said they were dressed that way
because they knew there weren't many women
in Inuvik and they wanted to impress
the few who were there by dressing like Big Shots

and I knew I was just like that
and I knew I was just like Chuck
so with all the kindness I could get in my voice
I said, You know, Chuck, you're just like that.
You're just like a white man from up south.

I know, he said.

IN HONOUR OF THE WOODY GUTHRIE MEMORIAL

Jan. 20/68

At this moment in Viet Nam
as I write this the clear moon I imagine
shines down on one peaceful scene.
It's night and the village sleeps.
Everything is quiet as the universe.
The moonlight lies everywhere
illuminating chance corners.

There was about to be an attack
but I've deflected it with this poem.

BEER AND PIZZA

It's Hiroshima Day and in the heat I lug a load of empties to the beer store.
It's too hot to think. I wait for my thoughts but they do not come streaming,
they never do when I wait for them. Even the bus is slow to come.
Civilization ended thirty-eight years ago today. That's a thought, but it
fails to convince. A skinny old drunk in a red shirt staggers under a load
of empties, crosses the gas station lot, drops one case, the empties roll
all over the lot, he yells out ah shit, people sit in their cars and watch and
smile, nobody wants to help him. I'd help him for sure but I've got two
cases of my own empties to contend with. So I yell across the street at him:
Make two trips! But he's too drunk to hear me. All over the world people
are drinking beer and thinking about Hiroshima, how the survivors
immediately after the blast speculated calmly on what the cause had been.

Swamp gas. A few nights ago someone torched the Women's Bookstore,
hoping to get the abortion clinic above. But the store was gutted, the clinic
untouched. And last night Sandy Segal phoned to tell me to get down to the
store, the local coven was having a purification ceremony. I'd been watching
a television program about spiders and when she phoned they were showing
a mother spider who shortly after the birth of her babies redirects her own
digestive fluids to turn her body into mush for the cute little things, and
her heart and lungs keep operating as the babies devour her body. When I
got there the women were sitting in a large circle amid candles, incense,
and were coincidentally chanting a hymn to the Great Spider: "You are the
web, you are the weaver." And they passed around a magic glass heart from
hand to hand and each woman who held it had to say a word about what the
bookstore meant to her. Frankly the comments weren't that interesting,
they were valedictorian in tone, and everyone was too nervous to sound
sincere. I wanted to tell them about my fabulous spider coincidence,
but by the time the heart got to me somehow they'd started chanting
again so Sandy and I looked at each other and decided to go for pizza.

THE SMELL OF WATER

The important thing is to keep
writing

I have taken a break from dull typing
to say this

for today I bought a new coat
& drove with my family to Burlington

& worried about my taxes
& my wife complained that a soup bone
now costs $1.85

& none of it is important
unless I write

for that is what I think
& I do not have to think that

but I do
because I want to

for my parents were television sets
& I am sending out my waves
onto this page

hoping you will turn your head
away

for I am covered with the smell
of water.

BOX OF THREE

1

In this house
small box
among a million
sound as Bach's
organ (Bach Sr.)
small perfection
perfect proportion
little Joan
littler Alison
& their cats
& birds & fish
& plants
           dance
thru dream
              & dream
thru dance.
              In
this house Joan
(I can see it after only
2 months) is growing
(more & more beautiful)
Alison is growing taller
more awake & graceful
& radiant & I'm
growing
fatter
      & fatter
& more blissful.

2

From this living room
I hear most any time
the roar of Kenilworth Avenue
2 blocks over
traffic jams
neon screams
polluted air
human supremacy
dogs laughing at us. In
1915 there were 3
houses (2 were vacant)
along the 3 miles
of Kenilworth Avenue
and 3 little factories
at the Bay end. This
was rural, man. People
were living & dying in
Hamilton without ever
having been as far out
as Kenilworth Avenue.
Even now it's village-like
self-contained
altho ruined twice a day
by rush-hour volleys
from the Mountain to the Bay
from the Bay to the Mountain.
Self-contained. I know old guys
who won't set foot off Kenilworth
for months at a stretch.
It's beautiful. I wish I didn't
work downtown, 4 miles in.

3

Thru the living-room
window I see
leaves of red
& gold blowing round
(you guessed it it's October)
some, with thin tendrils,
are hanging on to thin
branches of fat trees
& Joan says she's
always thought the leaves
amuse themselves with contests
to see who can hang on
the longest. And I tell her
yes in a previous life
I was the winning leaf
& know the feeling.
Stuff like that.

PICTOGRAMS BY STARLIGHT

Through the train-station mirrors the critics
Click their tongues and turn away.
It's true my clothes are old and baggy.
I look the sort of never do well
(Not dressed very well by New Zealand standards)
Who would read a book by a Western Samoan.
Which I am. Albert Wendt. Recommended.

Some invent what they write but there's no dream
Like the dream of whatever happens to be transpiring
In your mind in the moment. Impossible to capture
In all its thrilling brilliance. Each little thought
Bursting up through the cerebral sewer
Like baby cabbages or freshly washed socks.
Each one fresher than the one before,
Each one striving to be picked up and admired,
To be the centre of attention in a humdrum world.

Why am I here? So I won't have to be
Elsewhere. Seventy-five years ago Rilke
Pronounced the death of bourgeois travel.
It's like being back at the dawn of creation,
New Zealand still rising out of the waves,
Snakes and mosquitoes haven't arrived yet
And fresh volcanoes erupt with no warning.

Maoris with spraybombs do pictograms by starlight.
    Pictograms as perfect as those from antiquity.
       Many carry heavy books
With the names of their ancestors back to Eden.

The manager of a prosperous bookstore in Auckland
Tries to evict a Maori browser

Because he appears to be exposing himself.
Turns out his belt has a dangling end.
Yet all the best writers in New Zealand are Maoris
And the Maoris have the best fish-and-chip shops.
You never see them eating cold asparagus sandwiches.

At dawn milk trucks play dreamy melodies.
Passengers on buses sing along with the Muzak.
Bluebirds on fenceposts tilt their heads to listen
And sheep scamper uphill when a bus passes.
The whites are still proud of being white
But they dress as proper Americans might:
White belts, white shoes, pink shirts, lime trousers.
The sheep dotting every hill resemble angels.
Everywhere there's sadness, silence, seclusion.

THE SPOILED BRAT

I couldn't stand the little bugger. He
was a spoiled brat. But his mom & dad
were always nice to me. So when they
asked me to mind him I said okay.

About 10 o'clock I picked up his dad's
rifle & pointed it at the kid. "I'm
going to shoot you, Bruce," I said,
& he ran in the corner & started crying.

He didn't notice me pulling out the shells.

Then I pointed the rifle right at his nose
& pulled the trigger. It just clicked.
He stopped crying & smiled.

So then I made a big show of loading the
gun again & then I told him I was really
going to shoot him this time & he began
to cry again & I pulled out the shells
without him seeing me again but I guess
I must have left one of the shells in
because when I put the gun under his nose
this time & pulled the trigger the gun
went off & he fell to the floor with
half his head blown off.

A VERY CALM DEMEANOUR

2 sonnets for John Lennon's 61st birthday
Oct. 9/01

It's always good to be prepared for death
because of course it could happen at any time
(the Dalai Lama says we should live our lives
as if we're being stalked by a sniper)
but with gangs of terrorists bombing the USA
and Americans bombing Afghanistan
with pneumonic plague breaking out in India
and maybe China and Vietnam as well
travelling the airlines in the same way
as bubonic rats get around on ships
and civil wars raging all through Africa
where everybody who's anybody's a refugee
or an orphan of refugees or of AIDS
— a very calm demeanour is required.

Le Devoir says *nous sommes tous américains*
and Putin says humanity is maturing
but as for me I'd prefer to say that we're
an orphan growing up knowing his mother
died of AIDS and not knowing his father at all
except that he was a soldier who raped mama
while she was trying to flee a bomb attack
or we're starving to death and a humanitarian box
falls from the sky and lands in the danger zone,
there's enough pasta to last a week and also there's
enough penicillin to prolong a life or two
and we're crawling towards it and expecting
at any moment to be blown up by a mine
— a very calm demeanour is required.

WHAT DOES IT MEAN ...

To be afraid to look at a plane flying overhead in waking life for fear
that your gaze may cause it to explode in mid-air as planes always do
when you look at them in your dreams.

To be unable to recall anything about the first time you beat your
father at cribbage, but to remember every movie he took you to as a kid
— David Lean movies, Powell-Pressburgers, Charles Laughton, H. G.
Wells, *Kon-Tiki*, *Scott of the Antarctic*. You can even remember which
theatre each film showed in and where you sat.

To remember running home scared after seeing a stern image of
God in the clouds, then discovering in later years that every Protestant
Canadian kid had the same experience in those days.

To understand all of a sudden what a stranger in a train meant in a
brief but intense discussion you had thirty years ago in which he
predicted in a rough outline everything that would happen to you. He
said it was a hobby and he wasn't very good at it yet. It all turned out
true.

That when you're a kid you can never induce yourself to fall asleep
and continue a dream that has been aborted upon awakening, no matter
how desperately you wanted to find out what would have happened
next if your brother hadn't thrown a baseball mitt in your face and said,
Hey it's Saturday. But when you're an adult it takes no effort at all.
Could it be a central nervous system modification as a result of
exposure to digital laser technology? We fall asleep and the dream
resumes in exactly the same frame.

That our dreams know exactly what we need to see and hear but
they also know if it's too easy and straightforward it won't be valued.
Dreams and poetic fantasy are the media of prime subtlety: nothing
else is worth the focus.

To have succeeded in all the unimposed things that you privately
thought important as a kid to succeed in, but to have failed in all the
things that were imposed upon you and which you considered it your
solemn duty to succeed in.

To remember for such a long time the amusing subway smile of the old drunk who noticed your *Toronto Sun* and asked politely if you were finished with the Sunshine Girl page, the same old fellow you later saw sitting on a park bench on a sunny winter afternoon with his pants down trying to masturbate.

To be surprised every day at the strange things we remember and the stranger things we have forgotten for decades but with no warning may suddenly remember again.

* * *

The seven ages of the fruit fly:
Hour 1: Eat up all the fruit.
Hour 2: Fly around like mad.
Hour 3: Rest on the wall but be ready to resume Hour 2–like activities when a large mammal comes into the room.
Hour 4: Rest on the wall and forget about large mammals.
Hour 5: Fall to the floor.
Hour 6: Die.
Hour 7: Get swept up by a large mammal who resolves to keep fruit in fridge henceforth.

WALTER'S MOUSTACHE

When she met Walter for the first time, she touched his moustache lovingly and said, "Oh no, you haven't grown a moustache!" No, Grandma, I said, that's Walter, I'm over here. Her mind had sparked back, it appeared, to her first husband who'd been dead sixty years. In his photos he had a moustache just like Walter's. She'd been married fifty years to her second husband, but her mind had its secret flashbacks to her first. And her second entered the room as if he'd been reading minds again, and began speaking of her first husband, what a good man he was although they'd never met, how he was a pacifist, and never would have fired his rifle at another man, he told people before he left for France in 1917 that under no circumstances would he ever shoot at another human being, he could speak seven languages, he only went off to war because he didn't want to humiliate his parents by having everyone in that little Yorkshire town think he was a coward, and he was shot down in the first minute of his first battle and was killed. Tears were streaming down the old man's face, and it occurred to me he'd be dead soon and when he died husband one would be in heaven waiting.

Smiling, with a reassuring handshake. You have no idea the dreams you have when you're in your eighties, said my grandmother. People who've been dead for sixty years appear and you can see them so clearly you can almost reach out and touch them. And she reached out again to touch Walter's moustache. Her dim eye said she was thinking of husband one again and I wondered if husband two realized it and if it made him sad at all. No, by the time you've reached that age you've absorbed in your life so much sadness a little more sadness wouldn't affect you at all. They've witnessed the century to end all centuries, and yet still the seasons change, sadness accumulates and makes us wise, and we die to make room for the young, who are really the same as us all over again but in a different disguise.

SPIRITS BAY

New Zealand, May 13, 1987

1

Solitude sublime watching the sun
Sinking into the sea and the green
Waves queuing up for their tickets
To come crashing and rolling up the sandy beach
At the northern tip of the North Island.

Immense bay surrounded by solidified
Asteroids of lava with trees growing on top —
I dreamt of this bay three years before,
The volcanic islets breathing like lungs,
And I'm thinking of how we used to be friends
And how I don't give a damn anymore.
I've been chasing sandpipers along the beach
But now I need courage, I'm alone and afraid
Of night and the sound of the crashing waves
Amplified crazily in this nuclear coliseum.

Spirits Bay where the souls of the dead
Say adieu and plunge into
The radiant void of sea and sky.
Membranes separate thin cosmologies,
Each moment underlaid with a billion others.
Unimaginable ceremonies can be sensed
On such nights with warm moons rising.

A bomb lying on the beach for decades
Is about to explode under my feet.
A newborn volcano is about to erupt,
Just big enough to swallow a church and a graveyard.

I'm the last person on earth, so lonely
So naturally I want to go back in time
And join in whatever absurdities prevailed.
I open a discarded plastic bag
And a severed human head stares out.
And it has my face. Even the birds
Are filled with ecstatic superstition.

The face of the moon is serene and clear
Down here in the Southern Hemisphere:
Moonlit families of sandpipers
Skitter away at my approach
The moonlit lake behind the beach,
The moonlit island in the lake,
The moonlit globs of volcanic rock,
Awash in the thunderous moonlit waves.
Moonlight doesn't give a damn
And yet it somehow gives a hoot.

Things photographers never photograph
Everywhere I look. An invisible lighthouse
Twenty-five miles out at sea
Blinks through a small opening in the stormclouds
And a thin layer of pressed gold
Hovers above the horizon and swallows
The golden swordblades slicing obliquely
Down through the golden chinks in the cloud.
Finally I realize what a coward I am,
Afraid of the explosive crashing of the waves,
And I look at the sky for courage and pray.

2

Inanimate objects full of life.
An ancient Maori chieftain is floating

High above the waves, his eyes
Twin openings in the thunderclouds,
Openings through which the blue of the sky
Glows with the green of the setting sun.
He's a puddle of light in the Aotearoa sky
Reflecting the earth to which he's saying goodbye.
As he sails out over the Southern Seas
His eyes are rimmed with golden lights.
He allows me a glimpse of the flame of his heart
As he slowly dissolves into paradise.

The fierceness of his heart and his solemnity
Subdue the power of this bay.
As the strands of sunlight pour into the sea
His strength begins to pour into me.
From now on whenever I need courage
I'll have to remember this moment and the seahawks
Flying out of the dying warrior's eyes.

Emptiness that comes to all in time.

The more courage you have the more you need.
    Like everything else. The gods have a hold
        On the freedom that comes to all in time.
            If I came here looking for courage I'll leave
                Wondering what to do with the courage I've found.
        This chief in his agony must appear to those
    Who come here looking for him and tonight
I'm the only human on this stretch of coast.

There's no end to how much courage and sanity
You need before you can afford to surrender.
The old warrior dissolving with the obligation
Of facing death after a long life,
Of facing the morning after a long night.

THE ANGEL

I

Dear friend, for several weeks
I've tried to avoid writing
but tonight I read three little poems of yours
and saw you sitting in your lonely house at 3 a.m.
in a large city a thousand miles away
writing,
words lifting out of your
unselfish heart
and my own heart melted

and I opened the dusty door of my writing room
and wrote the above
then went out and made coffee
then returned and wrote the following

for there are many reasons for writing
and only one is acceptable
for it has come to pass
that everyone can read and write
and every day we abuse
the language
that was given to us
by the poets

II

I started writing the day I was born
and even now when my face has finally
begun to lose its boyishness
I find I have little to say
and little understanding of why

I continue
and I saw you sitting by your brown globe
in the 20th century, writing
not bothering to ask why
of the gentle spirits around you

III

I was driving along the 401
driving to the university
to give a poetry reading

but the centuries pressed in
and I was driving my old one-horse wagon
to market with a load of magic potatoes
from my magic garden.

And today the old blind violinist
who stands on street corners in Hamilton
with his tin cup
died

for thought is cheap and endless
and perhaps if he had thought about it
he would have quit in disgust
and applied for a pension

forgetting the child's terror
not wanting to pass the old man by
and having no money for the cup

so he taps the bottom of the cup
hoping the blind man will think
he'd received another coin

but he taps it a little too hard
and the coins from the cup
fly up in the air
and fall to the sidewalk

and the blind man continues
playing his sad violin.

IV

"Stop the bus, I'm going to be sick,"
my brother would call out
and he would get off the bus
and he would vomit at the side of the road
then get back on proudly, age 9.

I never got sick on the bus.

Today a short fat woman in a short
black skirt and a short black jacket
got sick on the bus.

I felt some meanness inside me
when she pushed her way on the bus
in front of me
but my meanness went away
and I began wondering
if her ancestors and my ancestors
had ever met
when I looked and saw
she was about to be sick.

She vomited neatly in the aisle
and no one said a word.

I was sitting with a book in my hand,
my finger marking my page
and I forgot the book, knowing only
my finger was in something important,
was stopping something dreadful from happening,
was preventing further language abuse,
and she vomited neatly in the aisle
as if my finger had been in her throat.

When I got off the bus another man
got off the bus and I walked behind him
watching his black shoes
moving along in the bright white snow
like typing on a page
knowing he too saw the woman vomit
and hoping it didn't bother him.

V

And for several weeks now poems I did not
want to write rhymed in my head,
poems I did not like, poems that made me sick.

I met a literary gentleman who said,
"But Irving Layton's poems are so pithy,"
and I objected, saying some of them are passable,
only later realizing he wasn't lisping.

I read several books by poets striving
for pithiness.

I felt like a lonely ant in an anthill.

Beethoven's symphonies sounded like
squadrons of trained ants.

People looked like ants.

They talked like ants.

They moved in swarms like ants.

The ants were everywhere.

I watched U.S. comedians on TV
mocking Russian ants and Arab ants
and congratulating themselves for
being able to laugh at their own antics.

I saw how corrupt I was.

I read three small poems by you
and an angel came out of my heart.

JANE AND JEAN

Jane dresses up as a vampire and enlivens an all-day prayer meeting at a cute little rose-covered Pentecostal Alliance church in Beowulf, Alberta.

Jean reads outrageous passages from Patricia Blondal's *A Candle to Light the Sun* to a committee of highly empowered teenage vegetarians trying to transform Toronto into a no-traffic zone.

Jane snowmobiles to an ice-fishing site in the Haliburton Forest and encounters timber wolves.

Jean makes friends with lonely housewives spending the morning reading newspapers in Tim Hortons donut shops in Fenwick, Fonthill, Dunnville, Fisherville, Smithville and neighbouring communities.

Jane stocks the Grand River with brown trout.

Jean enjoys listening to the Kingston Trio on the old jukebox at the Barmaid's Arms while exhibiting her informal charms over a game of NTN Trivia after a busy day peeking through the keyhole of the ladies' change room at Honest Ed's.

Jane strikes up a passionate friendship with Julia, the lonely and desperate prison dentist.

It takes Jean weeks to recover from the punishment given her by Jane for being overly optimistic about the future of their friendship.

Once back on her feet, Jean pushes a Vietnam war hero to the brink of suicide, then deliberately antagonizes the mob.

Jane, Shashi Kapoor and Claire Bloom get laid. Sly Fate and Princess Boo Hoo are dying to hear all about it.

Jean's attempt to appear hip and trendy at a celebrity party backfires.

Jane gets a bit part in *World's Great Animal Outtakes* and strives to tone down her quirky, gleefully gay manner.

Jean binges to reach 300 pounds so she can claim disability.

Jane goes on the trail of a mythical beast.

Jean takes up painting and becomes an eccentric, deeply passionate and free-spirited opium addict with a special interest in totem poles and other artifacts from a certain unnamed dying culture.

Conrad and Barbara struggle to adjust to Jane as their new aunt while keeping their real aunt's memory alive.

Jean calls Window Shade Supply at (905) 475-0943 for architectural specs.

Jane amasses the world's largest collection of quality tabletop frames and book-bound, acid-free photo albums.

Jean is offered over six million combinations to create a custom-designed couch that she knows would be one of a kind.

Jane clones her friend the prison dentist Julia's dead child's cells and plants them in her own womb.

Jean is frequently called upon to try to talk her prison dentist friend Julia out of killing her brain-surgeon father.

Jane becomes a glossy airhead, but fabulously popular owing to her discovery of anti-gravity bestiality.

People begin to whisper about Jean's terrible vanity and her cutthroat philosophy.

Jane's best friend, the Port Dalhousie hooker and former prison dentist Julia, dies in her arms after an orgy of prescription drugs and non-prescription sex with several retired veterinarians from Port Colborne, Port Maitland, Port Dalhousie and neighbouring communities.

Jean presciently prevents a stalker from killing a movie actress whose yet-to-be conceived daughter will become a Prime Minister of Canada.

Jane flies to New York with an Alberta businessman and his charming wife and has nothing but trouble for the next twenty-four hours.

Jean becomes cantankerous and causes problems for the guys when she becomes an overnight house guest.

Jane discusses art and spirituality with Bill Moyers.

Jean campaigns for affordable housing by sending Sheila Gostick look-alikes into the streets of Niagara-on-the-Lake.

Jean accompanies Crad Kilodney to The Bay for the five-buck roast-beef special and ends up losing five thousand dollars in penny mining stock investments.

Jane makes a citizen's arrest of a dozen Canadian army traitors planning to sell a superweapon to Quebec.

Jane prevents an unwed fertile couple from attempting to adopt a carload of baby seals.

For complex ethical reasons Jane refuses a large commission to adapt Merce Cunningham's 1991 play *Beach Birds* for prime-time television.

Jean spills a mug of hot cocoa on her lap from the shock of seeing Anne Murray, on TV, trying to boogie down.

Jane visits the addicts at a treatment centre near Toronto and listens to their pained attempts at explanation and self-discovery.

Jean sets middle-aged men's pulses racing.

Moses Znaimer interviews Jane and offers her a job running Citytv and Bravo!

Jean, who is beginning to bore, bother and bewilder her friends, makes a fortune teaching comfortable Afro-Canadians about racism.

Bravo TV airs an hour of Jane being interviewed by Moses Znaimer.

Jean suffers from the banality of life so she ups and cancels her cable TV subscription.

Jane advises her dangerous former college roommates, Princess Boo Hoo and Sly Fate, to start a tumultuous affair with a famous novelist from a distant country who is giving a reading at Harbourfront.

Jean sneaks away to the circus after her favourite soup vendor refuses to serve Mary with whom Jean has been having an affair in order to make Pamela Wallin jealous.

Jane specializes in difficult windows and cottage country applications.

Jean turns a night in front of the TV into an unforgettable adventure.

Jane loses her job as Moses Znaimer's secretary and is thrown in jail for being generally obnoxious about it all.

Frank Magazine publishes several photos of Jean giving all-night English lessons to several members of the Bloc Québécois.

Jane takes Princess Boo Hoo to seedy fading Owen Sound, the lakeside town voted most likely to epitomize patriotism, for a frisky weekend, but the Princess insists on taking an overdose of locally brewed Ecstasy and has to have her stomach pumped.

Jean becomes a streetwise reporter who can get the plain folks to open up to her.

Jane insists that company downsizing prompted her dismissal from Citytv.

Jean saves a bundle on a wide selection of beds, wardrobes, dressers, night tables and a brand-new line of value-priced Simply Country bedroom furniture.

Jane has always had the inside scoop on books people are talking about.

Jean's amazing abilities to spin milk and secrete venom result in medical benefits.

Newly licensed Jane has an automobile accident.

Jean has three dates for Saturday night, Princess Boo Hoo and Sly Fate have none. What to do?

Jane helps Bob Dylan and the Rolling Stones influence modern music.

Jean thoughtlessly takes a group of Down's Syndrome patients on a tour of the Witless Bay Ecological Reserve in Newfoundland.

Jane becomes inexplicably compelling and the easily shocked turn away from her.

Jean searches the Internet for pictures of Dolly Parton in the nude.

Jane is torn between having a threesome with her yoga instructor and Heather Reisman and continuing to repair the cracks in the cinder blocks.

Jean is seized by pirates who have been inbreeding for three hundred years.

Jane advises a philanderer's fiancée to turn their home into a massage parlour.

Jean wins a ten-gallon drum full of DMT when she comes third in a pinochle tournament.

Jane shows Moses Znaimer how to juggle domestic duties and deadline obligations.

Fortune erases Jean's memory at exactly the right moment, causing her to miss *both* the lopsided down-to-earth stories of the chaotic and comic world of Newfoundland taxi-man Calvin Pope *and* Moses Znaimer's thoughtfully rambling monologue on the Jungian philosophy of Robertson Davies.

Jane pries open an abandoned trunk and discovers irrefutable evidence that her uncle, ostensibly a barber, was actually a pioneer Socialist filmmaker who disappeared while collecting mushrooms in the remote and soggy lower Grand River valley in the early spring of 1934.

Rejected by everyone, Jean continues to drink mescal straight from the bottle, thereupon endangering lives when she gets behind the wheel of an idling police cruiser.

Jane tracks down the family of the donor of her sister's new lungs with hilarious results.

Jean is acquitted on all charges of supplying underage dancers to a Chicoutimi nightclub.

Two teens who suspect they might have killed their newborn baby make off with Jane's credit cards.

Jean becomes interested in the invisible world of butlers, waiters and salespeople.

Jane loses her self-control when an overnight guest turns into a werewolf under a full moon.

The pool man at Jean's health club wants to become her best friend.

Jane takes a job as a sultry singer and stirs up a savage gang war in Pamela Wallin's old neighbourhood.

Jean leaves her embroidered map of the Niagara Peninsula in a gift shop after having a sexy encounter with a beautiful bearded lady paraplegic who had a small role in *Broadway Danny Rose*.

Jane grants freedom of worship to all Christians.

Jean is the main witness at the inquest into the horrible accident that took the life of Chuckles the Clown.

Jane survives a bad patch by learning to express her emotions and by summoning warrior vampires to annihilate several men with designs on her inheritance.

Jean loses to Smoky and Sad at Scrabble and has to spend the afternoon tied to their bed, then the three of them fly to Nevada for the annual Bullnanza in Reno even though they're supposed to be on jury duty.

Jane is amazed to discover that Pamela Wallin, with whom she once considered having an intimate affair, now has her own TV show at 10 p.m.

Jean is forced to consider airing her dirty laundry in public.

Jane spends a lovely weekend visiting burn victims, torture victims, the parents of children who have suffered crib death and other people in agony.

Jean visits Hamilton, Ontario, as part of her ongoing search for Noah's Ark, and is thrown in jail after Mayor Bob Morrow tries to engage her in mortal combat.

Jane finds out what really goes on behind Bay Street's closed doors.

Jean proves that heavy-metal messages did not destroy the life of the son of an abusive father.

Jane serves blueberry-bean muffins and chocolate dessert to Hilda and Zelda who are trying to fix her up with a lifetime supply of Crunchy Granola.

Jean gets stomach cramps when eternal life is conferred upon her by vampire bees.

Jane thumbs her nose at ancient traditions and heads for tragedy in Atlantic City.

Jean is thrilled to be interviewed by Kildare Dobbs for a special *Ideas* installment on running from life's responsibilities.

Jane tries psychoplasmic surgery on a raging woman who has been experimenting with fertility drugs.

Jean goes into an ecstatic fit whenever anyone mentions Carlyle's book on the French Revolution.

Jane, after being inadvertently kidnapped, drugged and blindfolded by several members of the Vancouver city planning committee, is inadvertently rescued by a quartet of drunken merchant seamen when they inadvertently break into the main headquarters of the Fireside Reading Club.

Thrilled with having quit her boring job teaching Mennonite ministers to become role models for streetcorner glue-sniffers, Jean is struck by lightning while jumping for joy and dies with a gap-toothed grin on her face. But when Jane sadly goes to identify the body, Jean suddenly opens her eyes, leaps off the slab, throws her arms around her friend and says, "Oh, dear! I've just had the most glorious near-death ex— !" and then dies again. Jane is so sad she slashes her wrists, and then, still bleeding, converts to Catholicism and joins a convent.

THIRTY-FOUR LINES ABOUT HORSES

If you slice open the brain of a dead horse you'll often find
tiny hooves imbedded in the centre of each lobe.
From the tops of hills horses can see the sea.
When a horse first senses the approach of spring
he will place his lips three inches from the left ear
of another horse and stand like that all afternoon.
Horses stare at the road and never move their heads
even when trucks full of horses roar by.
It's bad luck to argue about horses.
There is a herd of wild horses on the moon.
When a horse is shot horses all over the world tremble.
A horse in Blind River, Ontario, has a small bank account.
There are no horses in British Columbia.
A lie about a horse is not a real lie.
Horses love cigar smoke.
A horse knows when you have bet on him.
In 1949, a pilot, having had an argument with his fiancée,
pushed her horse out of a plane flying over Toronto at 3,000 feet.
LSD has no effect on horses.
Horses love the smell of telephones.
Horses love to carry beautiful naked women on their bare backs.
Horses love to have their eyes kissed by nuns.
Horses dream they are horses.
The average horse wants to be famous someday.
Horses love people with bad breath.
Horses are proud of their beautiful bodies.
A horse will develop high blood pressure if you cut off its tail.
Horses like to fantasize about making love to whales.
Horses love to eavesdrop on human conversation.
Horses barely tolerate the chirping of birds.
A horse will go out of his way to avoid a Seventh-day Adventist.
Horses are particularly fond of pregnant women.
When a horse is shown pictures of beautiful mountains

its brain begins to produce theta waves.

Horses love to be visited by horses from other countries.

Horses hate it when you run your fingernails down the blackboard.

FLYING OVER INDIANA

It was a small four-seater plane
kind of Spartan
and I was sitting in the back
with my bare feet propped up
        on the pilot's seat.

The pilot was flying low
over a small city in Indiana.
The city was filled with parks.
The parks were filled with canals.
The canals were filled with swans.

"It's a nice city. Reminds me
of Hamilton fifteen years ago," I said.

"Or Vancouver last year,"
said the beautiful woman
at my side, amorously.

The Bishop of Hamilton
was piloting the plane.
Some strange insects
came out of my left foot
and fell on his lap as he flew.

He was disgusted but said
nothing and kept flying low.

The beautiful woman had a small
mirror. I looked in it.
I had a crown of thorns on my head
and blood trickling.

THE SKY AND I

I'm paying my mother a visit,
walking towards her house,
and the road, usually smooth
and open, has become broken
and partially closed, barricaded
by crews of construction workers —

On my left they're laying sewers,
on my right an old graveyard
is being ripped out for the foundation
of a new apartment building,
and they're piling up stacks of old
caskets, groaning in the sun,

sad old cosmic caskets in rows slowly
moving along a makeshift conveyor belt
past a blazing incinerator
into which their contents are dumped
then moving on into the casket factory
where they are refinished
and resold for reuse —

But I manage to pass through
and visit with my mother for an hour
then return the way I came,
chat with the sweating workmen
in fact ask little questions
about the age of the graveyard,
height of the proposed building —

And the world is full of sunlight
and I am full of spiritual light
walking along like that

and the sky is full
of mild electrical powers
as inside me I feel
springs going off

and the sky and I
are full of a voice, saying

PREPARE NOW FOR DEATH

as I continue walking,
thinking what a good idea.

OVER AT THE UNDERMOUNT

A June afternoon in the 20th century,
drinking beer at the Undermount,
at a side window, foam
sliding down the inside of the glass,
clouds sliding along beneath the blue sky,
pigeons building nests in century-old
cornices of office buildings.

                Through
an office window I spot a man working at his desk.
He has been working there for 100 years.

A piece of silver paper
zips across the patio
as if drawn by a tiny invisible
team of horses.

IT'S UNBELIEVABLE

for Joan, December 31, 1969, the 10th anniversary of our first meeting

1

The sky stretching out forever is me, is me, is me
it made my fingers, grew my hair, animates me
fills me full of light, makes me radiant.

For 10 years you have been in my life
for 6 1/2 you have been my wife
I'm not sure I know who I am
but on my altar you are my lamb
We'll teach each other to be free
then I'll knife you & you'll choke me
But you are the song our world doth sing
So take from me this pretty ring

2

This poem on the last day of the sixties, the people who died
this fall & early winter, were not destined for the seventies

> Bill Davies, 42
> May Mattice, 52
> Jack Kerouac, 47
> Joe Garner, 87
> George Glidden, 26

& the Flu Epidemic in Europe this week has killed hundreds of the old
   & weak
this ant heap of a globe, because we have a written language & art
does that make us superior to the ants?

                    Poor George Glidden, 26
married, father of three, highballing transport trailer loaded with paper
from St. Kitts to Hamilton, Queen Elizabeth Way, suddenly Whomp!
smashes into a stalled truck, no lights, no flares, falls out of cab
dead, on fire, driver of stalled truck not injured, rolling on ground moaning
in agony of his murderous stupidity.

                    Poor George whose son David
died last year, has died today, will not have to die tomorrow?
There is only one being & he dies every day forever, no abstractions.

Poor Lloyd Abbey whom I hurt so deeply with my own stupidity
& now he doesn't want to be my friend anymore.
I offered him my friendship when I first met him a year ago
not because he was a poet living nearby
but because I was immediately fond of his distinct nuttiness
& only lately do I discover that he's highly sensitive about his sanity,
me so insensitive I never noticed it before & I've been
as you say, Joan, so hard on his incomplete self-confidence
& I'm full of admiration for the firm completeness of his new hate
& full of loathing at my own lack of touch, but Lloyd
was equally hard on me, always mocking my meagre musical taste,
calling me politically naive, taking potshots at my beloved Beatles
but I should've noticed he couldn't take the returns & I did notice
but he so successfully concealed his pain
'til it all burst out.

Poor Jackie Davies, Bill's young widow & their little son Michael,
growing so strong in grief & broken dreams, Jackie telling how nightly
during normal sleep she & Michael visit Bill on the astral plane
in a cute one-room cottage somewhere in a warm climate.
Bill & Jackie had (have) loved each other for three years
& we have been together ten & that is not enough
sincerely I want to get to know you better
after ten years I'm just now beginning to get to know you

in a new way that is maybe very rare among lovers
or maybe common but it's new to us.

                                    I get confused
where you leave off & I begin & someday if I outlive you
I'll be trying to write a poem about your death
& I'll no longer be confused or maybe more so.

Little morsel of mortality, Joan, you sometimes get tired of life,
who doesn't? We're all very similar, even the animals are just like us.
Allen Ginsberg is only Adolf Hitler with the light turned up,
& I & the Great Snowy Howl are brothers.
                                    Lloyd Abbey & John Lennon
are tied by invisible chords of equal spirit, with a lead wall barrier
for the sake of growing complexity & joy of confusion
& there is a great day coming
                                    & we'll all be here to see it.

    3

The animals are just like us, that's no insult to animals or humans.
To understand what I'm trying to say read *The Golden Ass of Apuleius.*
Apuleius used to go around saying the animals are just like us
& no one knew what he meant so he wrote the book
which I read & thought about for half a minute
& it became obvious as eating when you're hungry
or sleeping when you're tired that the inner conscious natures
of a turtle & myself are pieces of the same thing.
It's all a big dream invented by myself, say I
& the turtle says the same thing about itself
& if both are right both are one
split temporarily in this dimension of illusion
& stationed at two different posts
& given two different jobs & taking it all in.

4

There's no nice way to die, but it's better if you're old.
It's awful to see children die, especially in war,
especially because of adult stupidity
& all around us children are dying
& people not born yet are being cheated at best.
In our three decades we've seen a continent destroyed.
Impossible for us to get to the year 2000, three more decades
under the present political/economic situation
unless certain miracles occur. There are
several miraculous possibilities necessary for survival
(even non-white survival) & even if survival itself
contains no hope we'll grab for it because of the children
or just for the hell of it.

Glory is a spray-foam rug cleaner &
Peace on Earth Good Will towards Man, even that
has become a sentiment rather than a rapturous
rupturous angelic symphonic pleading

& even if things do work out & everything comes back into balance
peace / technology / equality / industriousness / fertility / harmony
will there be any room left for love or is hate necessary for love
& will there be a place for poetry? Will there be any need
for the unnecessary arts, for the unregimented impulses?

If some kind of World Government finds itself in power
they might find it necessary to sacrifice the arts for 200 years
which will be the same as killing it forever —

the only hope is for a harmonious balkanization of the world
so what is stifled in one place may thrive elsewhere —
I wouldn't take the job of world dictator
& I wouldn't let anyone else take the job.

In the meantime there is music, love, good food for some of us
& the rolling spirit taking it all in for all time
& a billion strange little joys popping up!

MY OWN TRUE NATURE

Opera recordings first became available in 1949 while animal imagery
began to enter my dreams in 1969. Two dreams were so strange I made
paintings of them: a wild eagle sitting on my head, a wild bull with its
head cradled in my arms. These are the things true lovers tell each other.
I had a conversation with a herd of cattle, I followed a cow as it swam
across Lake Ontario, I was transformed into a mournful lion trapped
at the bottom of a deep dark well. Dreams urge us to be compassionate,
animals don't dream, they are okay without them, they live in the moment,
they don't bother with dreams or clothing. Trees and flowers seldom dream.
But since this is a poem about talking dogs and barking men I must tell you
that last night I was walking along a country road in the Slocan Valley and a
well-groomed well-bred Scottish collie the size of a small horse joined me.
His chin touched my shoulder as we walked along. He asked where I was
    going,
I told him just down the road a bit and then I'm coming back, he eagerly
asked if he could trot along beside me and I said I'd be delighted. As we
walked he said he thought humans were crazy to be always trying to
    improve
the world, it only made things worse, and he thought Zen Buddhism
was an instrument intended to drive the entire non-Japanese world insane.

I was on the collie's back, and we were trying to swim a powerful river,
the other side invisible in the mist. Later I was talking to a strange man who
confessed that he was really a dog. He rolled up his sleeve and
showed me his canine fur. He was nervously smoking Black Cat Filters. He
wanted to splash in a rain puddle there on the road but felt trapped
in his human role. He said he was seven but he looked at least forty-nine.
He certainly smelled like a dog, but you wouldn't have noticed it
unless he mentioned it, and he did, and he also smelled like a man.
He had that special smell of canine consciousness: dim, wet with saliva,
something you can feel but not describe. Yet superimposed was a
distinct human odour: dry, distant, full of thought, repressed to the
point of insanity, uncomfortably clean, a creation of the human language

he'd learned to use too well. I liked him, felt sympathy for his plight
which was mine as well, but I felt I liked that collie better, if I may be
permitted to express my likes and dislikes. And I remembered that Ernest
Hemingway's wives were always complaining because he never bathed,
never changed his clothes, never shaved. Always smelled of blood and guts.
I used to wonder how he could have killed all those beautiful animals and now
I know! It was because he was one himself! And in today's paper there's a
story from Russia about an elephant with a thousand-word vocabulary.

A SENTIMENTAL INTRODUCTION

Every day I sit for two hours
removing the poison from the ozone
and replacing it with spiritual light

so that people on the street below
will sometimes look up at my window
and smile, for I am a sponge
in the bath of urban life,
and there is neutrality about me
right down to the question mark that sits
throbbing like blue neon in my pancreas
and people who get close to me
say there's nothing to like, nothing to dislike.
Being with me is like eating plain yogurt.
I'm as lovable as an ion generator.

And this morning as I lay sleeping
the sun shone through my window
so that I dreamt I was in a snowstorm
and eating vanilla ice cream
then I walked down to the beach
where people were swimming and sunbathing
and when I awoke a pigeon flew through the window
and left a white mess in my coffee
then sat there criticizing me
for not ending my poems properly

and I told it the movie last night
was so good I couldn't take a moment
to go for a pee so I peed
in my empty popcorn container
and when I got thirsty I likewise
couldn't leave to get a drink

and so I drank the piss —
Too bad you weren't there, I said,
you could have had some,

and it flew away.

THE IGUANA WITHIN

We're all getting colder — faster. A few years ago most people could not think — for various reasons — about getting cold until they had at least gone through a few years of being hot.

It is different today. Many people get cold before they've had a chance to get hot, and this segment of the population is growing.

The Canadian Hot and Cold Institute says the group getting cold without having gotten hot is increasing three times as fast as the rest of the population.

About 11 per cent of the population is now completely cold and this figure is expected to rise to 15 per cent by 2011 and 25 per cent by 2031.

"It's as if a large segment of the population feels, with the Elizabethan poet John Donne, as if their hearts had become too great for them," says Faye V. Rapsiddy, a professor of the sociology of thermodynamics at the Hot and Cold Institute at the University of Tuktoyaktuk. Dr. Rapsiddy is also a published poet and member of the League of Canadian Poets.

"And of course if you take the 'r' out of 'heart' you have 'heat,'" she pointed out. "It's as if we are tiring of our essential mammalian warmth and are looking back fondly to our cool reptilian roots."

She found a significant rise in the number of people reporting their hearts felt like piggy banks bursting with gold coins. And on each of the coins was cold-stamped a symbolic representation of their greatest desire, something they wanted greatly but felt helpless to achieve.

"It's chilling to see how images from Donne's Elegies, written four hundred years ago, could apply so well to our sociological findings today," she stated in a recent policy paper entitled "Is Donne Done?"

"And yet Donne would have felt out of place in today's society, where most would coldly disagree with his position that he would, in spite of his despair, rather be 'mad with much heat than idiot with none.'"

AFTER READING SHIKI'S POEM ABOUT THE DEAD DOG FLOATING DOWN THE RIVER

Why do humans live so long?
The dogs I knew in my childhood
are all dead
the cats
the birds
and even that big black horse I used to ride
on Uncle Cecil and Aunt Clara's farm
is dead, and the farm is now a subdivision
and Uncle Cecil and Aunt Clara are divorced
but they're still alive

and the children I played with
are living quiet lives here and there
and I imagine them
fat
unhappy

and while I'm asking childish questions
how did I manage to be born in the
twentieth century
and why did I used to wake up at night
afraid to die
and hating everybody?

What happened to all that poison
that was building up inside me?

It's two-thirty in the morning
and on the street below
a man is trying to break open
the newspaper vending box
to steal the quarters

and whenever a cruiser goes by
he stops bouncing the box up and down
and pretends to be buying a paper

and then there's Shiki
dying at thirty-five
his stomach bloated with persimmons
sad because he knew
he would never read or write another poem.

LETTER TO MY FATHER

In the past couple of years my life has become
incredibly trivial. I have become what they call
a creative writing instructor in a small college in the interior
of British Columbia. I paste on my office door, to compensate,
serious pictures — the Beheading of John the Baptist,
news photos of political executions, tortured bodies,
racing cars going out of control and flying into the crowd —
and students are annoyed or maybe the security guards or cleaning staff
for when I arrive in the morning the pictures have been torn down.
The students want to know how to become poets, how to write poems.
I tell them to think of a line, any line, and write it down.
Something like this: A Zimbabwe farmer, following the revolution,
says his morale has been destroyed because he no longer has anything
to live for. Then think of another line and write it down.
Something like: Father, what's it like to be old? And if
these two lines suggest a third put that down too, and a fourth,
and a fifth, as long as you're not forcing your mind to be
involved in what you're doing. And I genuinely like these people.
That's what amazes me, my feeling for them as individuals,
but they complain about me: tell me I'm obsessed
with form, that I ignore content, that I'm unable to appreciate
their individual vision, that I'm an old windbag.
Yeah, to them I'm an old guy. Your little boy has become old
at least in the eyes of the younger students. Others, older,
have given me their hearts, a more than fair exchange,
and last month as my fortieth birthday came closer
I started to panic. I even thought of walking out, walking out
to the end of the Government Wharf with a shotgun
and blowing my head out over the cold waters of Kootenay Lake
so that people would say gee he killed himself on his fortieth
birthday and people would say *tsk* I guess he feared old age.
Don't be alarmed. I learned this from you. You know
my childhood memories are full of images of you as a

warm, soft, likable (I had to check the spelling, you always
said don't ever write a word until you know how to spell it),
witty, moral, and highly self-conscious individual. The only
sport you took an interest in was boxing, or pugilistics
as your father used to say. You were my model in every way
and today the image I have of myself is almost identical
to the image of you I had as a child.
But you never had illusions about humanity. You told me
never to allow myself to be fingerprinted
and never to put anything in a letter I didn't want
the whole world to know. Oh my!
And remember the sad look that came in your eye
when I in my high chair flicked a spoonful of Pablum
into your face, that face that now is my own, the same look
when twelve years later we sadly tossed Uncle Joe's photos
into the fire. For you life was wonderful
but individual human beings were not so wonderful.
Maybe that's what you meant when you told me the whole
is greater than the sum of its parts. Mind over matter.

And, father, do you remember the time you dropped the monkey
wrench on your toe? I guess your foot was bare, the wrench fell
from the top of the furnace, you were very brave,
I don't remember you crying or yelling, ever,
though I remember you sad lots of times.
So your foot was an awful mess, the doctor came
and bandaged it up, and as for me it seemed right somehow
that my father should drop a monkey wrench on his foot.
That was the sort of thing that adults do.

When you were my age I was sixteen, almost as old
as some of my students. And I imagine they see me much as I
saw you. Probably not true but you have to believe something
unless you want to dissolve into the universe, honey into honey.
I was discussing astrology and one of the students

said she was born under the sign of Aquarius and I told her
both my parents were Aquarians. She looked surprised
and said I bet you never got along with them. On the contrary,
I said, I love them very much and consider it a tragedy
I live so far from them and seldom see them particularly
now when they're getting on in years, although it's true
their lives are harmonious, they're in good health, and don't
really need me. You know me. My needs are small. I go where I think
I might be needed. And sometimes I feel needed here.
For eighteen years I saw you every day. For the next eighteen
I saw you every Sunday. And now I see you once or twice a year.
Someday, maybe soon, we'll be permanently separated by death.
But both of us know there is no death,
just as there is no life, there is only us,
all together, all the time, for all eternity,
in a kind of incredibly intelligent and compassionate light
which is for now just outside our little minds.

Father, I know little of your sorrows, your fears,
although I know you have your share of them.
But as much as one human being can care for
another human being I will always care for you.

DARRYL & THE MOOSE

for Al J. Plant

There was a fat kid in there
about 12, with a bottle of pop
& a chocolate bar, & leaning
against the cooler.

           And I said
Excuse me, opened up one side
of the cooler. Just big bottles
in there, so I closed it, opened up
the other side, looked in, pausing,
hesitant.
           So the kid said What kind
are you looking for? And I said Oh
no particular pop, just whatever
looks good,
                then grabbed a Grape Crush.

As I opened it, two women, in their late
40s or so, walked in, flashing
big smiles at the kid, saying
Hello Darryl, then talking to the
woman behind the counter, softly,
the kid straining, listening like mad.

It was hot in there, so I dropped
12 cents on the tray & walked out.
Standing in front of the store,
taking swallows of pop.
                I'd had
enough when half finished, but didn't
want to take it back in like that,

so I finished it off dry, walked in,
plopped the empty down on the cooler.
Mom, said the kid, interrupting
the women's chatter, you owe
this man two cents.

        And she
got real flustered, looking about,
confused, then rang up the register,
smiled, put down two cents, saying
Thank you.
        And I flipped the pennies
& caught them, walking out past
Darryl. Just as I passed him I
winked,
        with a little smile.

And he smiled. God, did he smile,
little fat kid.

———————

Next door was the Moose Hall, and
on the step was sitting an old man,
nice clean-looking old man, the janitor
I thought, the doors open behind him.

I said Do you work here? And he said
Yes. And I said Do you mind if I use
your washroom? And he said Sure, it's
right down the stairs on your right.

And it was black down there, I couldn't
see a thing. So I came back up,
said Where's the light?

                    And he
answered It's just inside the door
on the left wall, about chest height,
well, you're taller than me, about halfway
between your chest and your belt.
                              So I
found it okay, & peed. And there were
some posters on the wall advertising
the Moose Lodge, & Mooseheart Village
and other things about the Moose.

Later, I was asking the old guy about
Mooseheart, & the posters, & the Lodge.

Mooseheart is a wonderful place for kiddies,
he said. It's just outside Baltimore.

Who can join this Lodge? I asked.
Oh anybody, just anybody, he said.
It's interdenominational, he said.
(I thought that was a pretty big word.
It wasn't on the posters.)
Anglicans, Presbyterians, even Protestants.
Doesn't matter about race, creed or religion.
Anyone can join. Anyone. But no niggers.

Whaaa? I said. In Canada?

The headquarters, he said, is in
the States, & when they say no niggers
they mean no niggers. I've been in

this Lodge for 52 years, he said,
& I didn't know about this till
just last week. I was wondering
why we never advertise our dances,
so I asked Ken (the bartender). And he
told me that if we advertised the dances
we'd get niggers, and that's against the
rules. Headquarters says no niggers.

He was a real nice old guy, though,
sitting on the step, in front of the open doors,
late midsummer afternoon 1966 in Hamilton.

FOUR EXPERIMENTS

1. *An Experiment with Debussy*

It was a family picnic.
They were sitting on a cliff
overlooking Lake Ontario.
Debussy's Rhapsody for Clarinet
was on the radio.
The wind was continually shifting
and making odd patterns
on the surface of the water
far below.

One of the children got too close
to the edge of the cliff. She fell.
Fortunately at the place where she fell
there was a relatively gentle slope
and she wouldn't be seriously hurt.
The girl's father was careful
not to alarm the others
as he was the only one
to notice her fall.
He quietly walked to the place
where she had disappeared
then began to climb down
searching for her.
He had a hard time finding her.
He began to worry.
When he got down to lake level
he was surprised to find
a large stone mausoleum
standing on the shore.
He went in looking for her.
It was a special mausoleum

housing the remains of children
who had died in the concentration camps.

Each crypt was surmounted
by a photo of the child
whose remains were inside
also a brief biography
was printed beneath each photo
like at the back of an anthology
of junior poets.
There were several mourners.
One had thrown himself
on the floor where he was rolling
over and over
and moaning like a sick
dog. Also he was bashing his head
on the floor and speaking
in tongues. It was terrible.

The father continued searching
for his daughter.
The mausoleum
was much larger
than it seemed from outside.
It seemed
to go on forever
like this poem.

When he found his daughter
he led her silently
back up the cliff.
She was not hurt.
He did not need to help her
in climbing back up the cliff
for she was quite athletic

for her age, seven.
In fact he did not even look
behind him
to see if she
was keeping up with him.
He knew she was.
He was confident,
almost supernaturally so.
When they rejoined the picnic
no one seemed to notice they'd been missing,
nothing was said about it.

2. *Three Cows Standing in a Pond*

It seemed as if he were on
the other side of the world
but he was only on
the other side of the pond:
my older brother
[or was it me?].

He had caught
a small catfish
and kept casting his line
fish and all
back into the water
to capture the thrill of the
catch over and over
like a cat tossing
a dead chickadee
and pouncing on it
again and again.

Finally his line
[or was it mine?]
got caught
on a branch
of a dead willow,
the fish hanging from the tree
like a tiny Christ.

I couldn't catch a fish
so I hid behind the bulrushes
and smacked the surface of the water
with the tip of my pole
making a loud noise.

I had one but it got away,
I yelled across the pond
and some cows came through
a hole in the fence slowly.

Three of the cows were standing
in the middle of the pond.
It was kind of insulting
because in our small minds
the pond was mysteriously
bottomless
at least in the middle.

One of the cows
headed towards me
its sharp horns glistening
in the hot sun
its nostrils quivering
with what I thought
was rage

and I ran up to the road.
I fished from the bridge.

It was a hot afternoon
and the farmer and his friend
were dressed in black suits
and white shirts, no ties.
It must have been a Sunday
in one of the last summers
before television was introduced
to Southern Ontario.

The farmer and his friend
chased the cows out of the pond
and back up through
the hole in the fence.

The farmer and his friend
were laughing with malicious glee
as they tossed a stick of dynamite
into the pond, when everything
went hot and still again
a large fish was floating
on the surface, the big old fish
we'd been trying to catch all summer.

My hands smelt wormy.
I had diarrhea.
I went in the farmer's outhouse
then I went in the tall grass
then I washed my hands
with sandy mud from the pond's edge.

Two big guys came out of the woods,
and I was scared for I knew them
and they were tough.

There was Bob who had a deadly
air pistol with capsules of heroin
hidden in the hollow handle.
He said the Mounties were after him
and a few years later he was killed
by a police car while walking
along the highway at midnight
not far from the pond.

And there was Henry who was
younger than me and shorter
but stockier and tougher.
He wrestled with me and beat me.
You're older than me but I can
beat you up, you sissy, he said.
I let him win though because I
didn't want to hurt his feelings.
He had a girlfriend named Brenda Snow.
He said: It sure is hot today but last night
I was in six inches of snow.

My brother said let's go but Bob
pointed the gun and said
Stay or I'll fire!

Bob is dead now as I said before.
Henry is now a hairdresser
in some small town on the Prairies
after spending five years in prison
for killing a cop on Christmas Eve.

Henry and some friends
were having a Christmas party
and the cops were recording
licence numbers of cars parked outside.
Just for a joke the cops
started letting air out of the tires.
The guys came out and started
fighting with the cops.
The guys were mad because they were
just having a normal Christmas party
complete with presents and a nice tree.

One of the cops drew a gun
and one of the guys grabbed it.
Several shots were fired
and a cop was killed
as well as one of Henry's friends.

The fight was on a gas station lot
and when I pass the lot now
sometimes I remember
and sometimes I don't.

As for the pond, it's still the same
but the dead willow has been removed
and the cows are all gone,
the farm's overgrown and vacant.

The road to the pond is the same —
gravel, but enough bare spots
so you can walk along it
fairly comfortable in bare feet.

And I feel sad about Henry.
Everyone told me what a crooked

bastard he was, loan shark,
pimp, drug smuggler, rounder,
parasite, Mafia punk underling,
but when I sold him my old
Sunbeam Talbot
I trusted him for a month
and when the month was up
he paid me every cent
he promised.

3. *An Experiment with Tim Horton*

There was a small tuft of human hair
at the sticky end of the toothpaste tube.
I plucked it out and flicked it to the floor.
It landed at the precise point
where four tiles touched.

His face was lopsided
like a clock at 7:05
and becoming more lopsided by the minute.
He had short legs like Toulouse-Lautrec.
He had crutches. I knew immediately
he was Jesus Christ in disguise.
He came down the aisle on the bus
and accidentally brushed against someone
and said excuse me. He
sat down behind me and began coughing.
I moved ahead a few seats
so the germs wouldn't land on the back of my head.
I could feel the vibrations of the wheels in my spine.

I was standing on a ladder picking apples
and looking out to sea.

I saw an Eskimo on a kayak
harpooning a narwhal.
At first I thought the narwhal
was vomiting but on looking closer
saw it was his tusk.
The narwhal's tusk
extends from the left side of his jaw
like a man with a toothache
eating with one side of his mouth.

It is Christmas in a typical
Canadian supermarket
and on display among the waxy fruit
is a box of small cacti all in bloom.
The sun did not rise this morning.
Never again will it move across
the long perfect skies
in slow soft strokes.
There is a small price sticker
stuck to each plastic pot.

It is midnight and in the
supermarket parking lot
a cop is in his cruiser
eating his lunch
though his break
isn't for another forty-five minutes.
He eats his four egg-salad
sandwiches with little thought
for the box of blossoming cacti
on the supermarket shelf.
Soon he will drive
to Tim Hortons for a coffee,
Tim Horton the famous hockey player
who was killed in a high-speed crash

while being chased by a cop
along the Queen Elizabeth Way
near St. Catharines
but still his chain of all-night
coffee and doughnut shops
continues on without him
and still the cops
are his most frequent customers.

The two girls were dear friends.
They were sitting at a table
in a Tim Hortons doughnut shop,
facing each other, exchanging
Christmas gifts. It was
Christmas Eve.
They were both thin and slightly
more than medium height.
They talked about food.
Meatballs with a marvellous tomato
sauce ... She makes an excellent paté!
They had musical voices. They were
each about twenty, very much alike.
But they did not look alike.
One had a large nose. The other
had almost no nose at all.

There were three cops sitting
at the counter drinking coffee.
Suddenly a fourth burst in, and all
four went zooming out.
They hopped in their cruisers
with lights flashing, sirens wailing —

A fifth had just been shot
on a gas station lot.

4. *An Experiment in Necrophilia*

I strapped the shovel
to my bicycle
and rode through the rainy
night

to the graveyard

where my parents
grandparents
and several aunts
and uncles
were buried.

I had an urge to see
what they look like now
each having died
in different years

although there are no
vintage years
I suppose
for death.

I intended no sacrilege
for I loved each of them while alive
and cherish my memories of them
and have spent hours
puzzling over them.

And when after much
sincere effort
I had each coffin
lying on the grass

its lid hinged open
the soft rain falling in
if anything I felt
the old folks
were slightly grateful.

I kissed each of them
where their lips would have been
had they been alive

and in each case
tried to remember
the last time our lips had touched
and thinking ahead
to the next person my lips would touch
and even farther ahead
to the last person my lips would touch.

And by the time they were safely
reinterred
I was exhausted
and I felt the sleepless nights
that have been plaguing me in recent years
would never plague me again.

PEACE

Joan, you won't remember this, but twenty years ago today you took my car
  out
for a spin with no oil and burnt out the engine. Cost me two hundred
  bucks.
It's all right here in my diary, though I can't remember what car it was.
And an apartment building exploded in Greenland killing all the tenants.
We went to see *I Am Curious (Yellow)* and you said it wasn't boring like
all the critics said it was. I was making $178 a week as a night proofreader
and the editor offered me a raise to $185 if I'd become a police reporter.
We had to borrow ten bucks from your mom for groceries. I took the job.
Jack Wilson died of stomach cancer. He was ten years older than we were
then and ten years younger than we are now. (Mocking chronology.)
Two days before his death I went to visit him in the hospital and read him
some poems from Al Purdy's new book. He liked them and said if he had
  his
life to live over he'd be a poet. Remember how funny he was? And his
pencil-thin moustache? He managed a little toy store at the shopping
centre where the race track used to be. I took Jennifer to John Boyle's
studio in St. Catharines and we bought his "Spanish Heel" (which I
still have) on credit. When I missed a payment or two he sent some Hell's
Angel guy to call on us. For Father's Day you bought me a pair of brown
Wellingtons. For your birthday I bought you a silver tray. In the middle
of the night I'd wake up feeling you'd been having a sneak affair with
Victor Coleman! I was annoyed with myself for having told Glenn
  Sinclair
my salary! My first byline appeared in the paper and my mom said to her
friends, Did you notice it was my son who wrote the story? I asked Alison
how she got so funny and she said she learned it from Jennifer. You asked
Alison why she was giggling so much and she said, "Because I got a big
joy." Dick Sherman wanted you to pose in the nude but you were too
much of a prude and now he's dead and can look at you in the nude
any time he wants from the spirit plane. Lots of entries about your
early interest in Bliss symbols and handicapped children, your weekly

visits to the hairdresser, your hour-long phone calls with your mother three times a day, your being annoyed because I was late coming home, and a beautiful loving note you put in my diary for me to see the next day or the next decade, in which you call me "the world's best husband."

I tried. What gets me is the energy! We were always so furiously busy! Everything's so peaceful now, isn't it? We have our loneliness, pain and guilt that will never entirely disappear, but there's so much peace!

MONKEY ON MY BACK

After Baudelaire's "Chacun sa chimère"

Under a vast grey sky in the nineteenth century, on a great dust-swept
plain, without roads, without grass, without a thistle or even a nettle,
I met a bunch of unearthly weirdos walking along with bowed heads. God,
the things I see! Right away I knew this would become transformed into
a great poem, and perhaps eventually would become my most famous! For
each of these guys was carrying on his back an enormous and ferocious
monkey, heavier than a sack of coal, heavier than all that stuff a Roman
soldier had to carry everywhere he went. And each monkey held on to its
poor host with all the force of its strong and supple muscles, each glued
itself to the man's chest with two huge clawed hands, and each held its
moronic face over the man's head like one of those horrible helmets worn
by ancient soldiers who hoped thereby to terrorize the enemy. So I went up
to one of these men and asked him quietly where he was going with such an
unusual burden. He looked at me as if I were nuts, said he didn't know what
the hell I was talking about, and he kept on walking, didn't miss a step, and
I could get nowhere with the others either. They just looked at me dumbly.
But it was evident they were going somewhere since they had such a great
aversion to stopping. And so they kept on walking. And I watching.

And thinking. It was curious that not one of these travellers seemed to be
bothered in the slightest by the ferocious beast hanging from his neck
and glued to his back. It seemed that each one thought of his beast as
being part of himself. They looked tired and their faces were serious
but there was no despair, and under the grey and depressing dome of the
sky their feet kept trudging through the dust of a country more desolate
than heaven, walking with the horrendous resignation of those condemned
to continue endlessly to hope. And the little parade eventually passed
and continued on towards the grey horizon, to the point where the long
line of the earth disappeared, and for several minutes I kept scratching
my head, trying to understand this mystery. But soon my irresistible old
friend, Dr. Indifference, lowered himself on to me, and I wandered off.

MY WORDS/HAMILTON

This is the 20th century speaking.
I think I made a wrong turn somewhere.
I was reading a book I didn't understand
& I remembered what good friends we were.
You dropped your children off at my place
& I raised them for you.
When you came back after the war
you settled in another settlement.

Your children are grown up now
& living in a third settlement,
neither the one in which you are settled
nor the one in which I am settled.

Yesterday I painted a picture
of Robinson Crusoe.
I remembered when you said
we were friends in Chaucer's England.

So many things have happened
but I have never been unhappy.
I was directing traffic at an accident
& stepped in someone's brains
& wasn't sick.
I have never been afraid of time.
It has always been like that.

We had some trouble with your youngest
in 1969. She wrote this poem

    Birds can fly
    Butterflies can fly
    Why can't I fly?

Then she became sick.
She was in a coma for six weeks.
For a year she did nothing
but draw pictures of horses
devouring each other.

Then she began spying on me
& writing letters to the police.

Now it is 1973, & she
is the *Vancouver Sun* food editor.

I know I have deeply offended you
but please get in touch with me.
You can dictate your life story
& I will type it out for you.
Send me your old clothes
& I will make new ones for you.
Send me a snapshot of yourself
& I will paint you transfigured
with divine ecstasy.
I want to get over this fear
not of dying but that I am dead.

These are my words.
They existed before I was born
but not in this order.
Before I wrote these words
these words were even then my words.

Dear friend, these are my words.
If you write do not use any of them.

IT WOULD BE NICE TO GO TO HEAVEN WITH YOU

for Ronn Metcalfe, 1930-1969

Chick Webb died in 1939 —
    tuberculosis of the spine —
& young Elephants Gerald
    took over the band.

Two weeks after Webb's death
they recorded "Stairway to the Stars" —
an extra emotional rendition
the brass so beautifully bold
& the reeds sort of fumbling.

All this on the radio in 1969
preserved as all knew it'd be.
I'm listening with gentle serenity
& the cat is resting at my feet
his head cocked & ears erect

& all I want to say is
this cat is listening too.

ELEPHANTS

Knoxville, San Diego, Winnipeg, Buffalo, Granby, Toronto: a list
of zoos I've visited this year. And anyone could see the gorillas at the
Toronto Zoo were conscious, deliberate philosophers with no vocabulary,
sitting in the glass house pondering ambiguity, paradox and the absolutes.
At Granby the gorillas were of a decidedly lower class. I hope they don't
read this. Two big ones studiously ignored a tossed banana for several
tense minutes until finally the male broke down and flickered with
interest and the female leaped from her perch, pounced on the banana,
then ate it herself while the male tried to pretend he didn't care. And
an American eagle attacked his mate over a gerbil tossed in their cage.

Viciously too, all heaven in a rage. But when I held out a handful of
nuts to the bull elephant he took only half, then slowly backed up so his
mate could have the remainder. The eyes of these sad spiritual lovers in
leg chains checked to see if I understood and appreciated their little gesture
of kindness and love, and I felt I'd been blessed by the Pope. They knew
there was nothing I could do to free them, though when two doves were
presented to Pope John Paul II in Montreal he released them and they
didn't fly away, just sat there in transcendental splendour in the middle
of crowded Olympic Stadium, little haloes radiant. And people who live
in the vicinity of the Granby Zoo when you get to know them will shyly
confide in you that late at night after they turn off the television they lie
in bed listening to and feeling the earth and sky quivering and murmuring
with the mammoth heartbreaking hour-long orgasms of the elephants.

MOONKAT

The face of the moon as one grows old
And one's friends begin to die
Begins to look warmer and more alive.
In the Southern Hemisphere the moon's serene.

In the shallow waters of a lagoon
Somewhere south of Fiji, the moon,
Chubby as a checker, as a billionaire,
Somehow has lost its horrified stare.

Knights need to keep an eye
Out for damsels in distress
And poets for spirit trapped in matter.
Overheard in a Suva bar
Where weary exiles drink Black Russians:
"Mr. Velikovsky, how are you?
And how's your mother's amnesia?"
"Oh, she's been over that for so long
She doesn't even remember having had it."

But your humble poet's in Los Angeles
    Where hummingbirds buzz and the black sage blossoms.
        Along with four black cleaning ladies
            At the end of their shift I'm waiting for a bus.
            "There sure are a lot of pretty girls
                In Los Angeles," I say, reminding myself
            Of Lucien in *Les Illusions perdues.*
        They look and laugh and one replies:
    "Yeah, and you ain't seen none of 'em yet!"
"I was freezing yesterday in Toronto," I say.

A blond starlet in a white Mercedes,
Licence plate MOONKAT, looks at me,
Slows down thoughtfully as if she's considering
Offering this gentleman a lift up to Hollywood.
But she changes her mind and accelerates.
The black women stand there tenderly smiling.

As soon as you save damsels in distress
They get themselves in distress again.
You have to keep on saving them over and over.
They're famous for it. But the rewards are great.
There's a sense of accomplishment.
Life would scarcely be worth living
If damsels didn't get in distress.
And where would we be if spirit wasn't
Continually becoming trapped in matter?

I float on my back in that warm lagoon
Thinking of friends who have passed away
Hoping up there among the stars
There's a planet as beautiful as ours
And hoping the people appreciate it
At least as much as we do flowers.
We sit naïvely on hilltops watching
The moon sinking behind other hills
Or into the sea and there's never a doubt
That all we're looking at is ours.

LAST CHANCE TO HIT BALLS
(Six Tanka and Six Haiku)

I apologize
For getting mad at the guy
  Selling stale apples.
He said he watched me stalk off
Punching my head with my fist.

When I was sixteen
George Meyers said my hips were
  Shaped like a woman's.
I almost died. Now I wish
I'd bought a dress and makeup.

Reading *Kokoro*
In the noodle joint. Waitress
  Notices and smiles.
Says she found it too slow but
It's her mother's favourite book.

Sixteen peaches sit
Ripening slowly on the
  Branch of my window.

If I couldn't be
Me I'd like to be either
  John Wayne or my mom.

Got a card from George —
He's in Capetown meeting with
    Batman, Superman,
And several other guys I
Met in Montevideo!

    Sometimes I think I
Invented the universe
    But that's silly, no?

    Whether or not we're
Sports-minded we all perhaps
    Have our own secret
Batting averages, win-loss
Records and sense of the crowd.

    I am a king who
Has three daughters, a daughter
    Who has three sisters.

    That busboy knows his
Beeswax, at first I thought he
    Owned the bloody joint —
Next thing I know he's doing
Backflips up and down the bar.

    There are wonderful
People in the world but I'm
    Not one, nor my friends.

Last chance to hit balls
For five hundred and twenty
Miles. (Sign in *Tin Cup*.)

TITLES I HAVE HEARD OF BUT NOT READ

Dreams have become so full of perfect intricate detail
& yet evaporate upon getting up —
Went up in a balloon thousands of feet above Niagara Peninsula
& jumped out with a parachute going down through cold wet clouds
& landing in Midway of Beamsville Fall Fair —
Went up again, took my father up this time,
& he pretended amazement at how well I could handle balloon's controls —
meaningless dreams, just for fun.

& this would make a good short story:
Going through familiar territory & suddenly
came across a store, combination garage & general store
that I knew had been torn down 15 years before —
Saw traffic but not much but what traffic there was:
cars over 20 years old looking new —
Garage was locked up, went into general store
& all the stuff just smelled & looked like 20 years ago,
remembrance of tiny things I'd never remember —
Checking prices, going through small wooden bins of perfect detail,
detail so perfect I never dreamt I was dreaming,
I figured by some sad loop I'd landed in 1953,
asked fat happy storekeeper's wife what year this was
& she threw her arms around me & laughed
& said You mean you don't know what year it is?
& her daughter & son-in-law called out from the back room
It's 1949!

Later, Jack, Al & me drove around checking details of 1949
trying to make sure no one was playing a joke on us.
Went down to Lake Erie, water was clean, beach was clean —
Everywhere we went we questioned people, cross-examined them,
asked if they'd ever heard of Elvis Presley,
hummed "Let It Be" for them, all of that,

went to a movie, sat in balcony of old-fashioned movie house
while old-fashioned horror movie was playing
& people fainting all around us.

Later went down to Joan's old neighbourhood
around Barton & Kenilworth,
saw her young mother & father, happy in prime of life,
then saw little Joan 9 years old sitting on curb,
then went around to Main & Kenilworth area looking for 9-year-old me,
4-year-old Jack & Mom & Dad in their early 30s —

Suddenly we were back in 1970 —

GREASEBALL

You glance at the motorcyclist who's just passed you
driving north out of Nanaimo
and you notice his right leg is horribly misshapen
and his pant leg is rolled up to his thigh
exposing a horrible scar
that twists around the upper leg
like the annulus of a mushroom
and his lower leg is shorter than it should be
and extends outwards strangely
for there is no knee with which to bend it
and there are only three toes on the foot.

You figure he's injured his leg in an accident
and is quite brave to be riding again
for it looks as if he's lost his leg
and had another grafted on
although that's crazy
but soon he is lost to sight
and you think no more of him.

Until you stop at a gas station
and while your tank is being filled
you go into the garage to price tires
and there is the same motorcyclist
washing the floor with a mop
and along with him
is a younger man
and the younger man
has a similarly misshapen leg
and his pant leg is similarly rolled up
showing an identical scar
the same missing knee
the same three toes.

And the younger guy has a dog
and when you nervously go to pat the dog
the dog growls.

Easy now, Greaseball,
calls out the younger fellow
as he opens a package of liver
and tosses it on the floor
and the dog jumps at it
and starts eating it

and there is the most beautiful smell
of lilacs in the air.

SEX WITH A SIXTEEN YEAR OLD

What I hate is being in a bar and a
beautiful woman squeezes in next to you
and you strike up a wonderful conversation
with a lot of vertiginous eye contact
and just when you think you might be falling in love
some big tough-looking guy shows up
with a nasty scowl on his face
and the woman sighs and gives you a sad look
and whispers *adios mi amigo*

Also I hate it that you are flying off
to Vancouver this afternoon
just as I am getting interested in you
which is unusual for me because
I never get interested in anyone under forty
and you're only sixteen. Sixteen! I know I
refused to go for Chinese food with you last night
because I figured there was a danger of us
ending up in the sack and you only sixteen
how could I have ever forgiven myself
and what if my daughters ever found out

And today on the phone you give me
a few more tantalizing details about your
seemingly extensive and far-ranging
sex life and you happen to mention you're a big
noisemaker
                    when you get going you wake up
neighbours dogs cats birds for blocks around

And all of a sudden I realize I should have
gone with you last night for Chinese food
I love noisemakers

they're my favourite people
but it's too late and the next time I see you
you won't be sixteen anymore

Sixteen come to think of it
isn't all that young the little woman
Charles Dickens left his wife and eight kids for
was not much older and Lauren Bacall
(when she put her lips together and blew
in *To Have and Have Not*)
was only sixteen
and Bogie who took one look at her
and decided to devote the rest of his life to her
was three times her age
four times would be scandalous
but three times is okay

PERCEPTUAL ERROR

He looks like a man who somewhere along the line has made a fundamental
error in his life, like everyman in other words, but unlike most men he is
lying naked in a snowbank at Spadina and Bloor reciting lines from Allen
Ginsberg's "Howl" in a calm voice. A pair of cops pick him up and throw him
in the cruiser. A stern-looking woman approaches me, I know she's going
to ask for a dollar for a hamburger so before she does I reach in my pocket,
get out a handful of change, and hand it to her. She's surprised but she
won't let on, and the change falls through her hand and lands on the sidewalk.
I bend down and pick it all up and put it in her hand carefully this time.
Suddenly I'm driving through Southern Alberta and there's a thunderstorm
in the sky to my right, another thunderstorm in the sky to my left, but the
sky in front of me is clear and full of stars. It is midnight and the lights
of a small foothill town twenty miles away can be seen on the horizon and one
of the lights keeps getting brighter then dimmer then abruptly as my car
climbs a rise in the road the light flies up into the sky and I realize it
isn't a light from the town at all but the tip of the crescent moon, and for
miles as I drive that hilly road through Southern Alberta the moon dips up
and down, slides up and down, appearing and disappearing behind the horizon.

Halfway through the second part of a Greta Garbo double bill the audience
starts hollering at me to leave, they can't hear the soundtrack because I
can't stop coughing. I stumble out to the lobby to get some cider and the
snackbar is closed but there's a little sign saying help yourself and a plate
in which to leave the money. I get a cup and open the cider tap but it breaks
off in my hand. So I run across the street and get some cough drops then go
back in to sit without coughing and continue contemplating Greta's wonderful
nose, wondering if she's still alive and if so where is she and would she
like it if I wrote and asked her to tell me the story of her life so I could
write it up in a book. At movie's end I take the broken tap to the manager with
the intention of apologizing for breaking it and offering to try to help him
fix it or failing that I'd be glad to pay for it but before I get a chance he
starts yelling at me in front of the people who were earlier yelling at me.
Why did you try to get cider when no one was here? he yells, mad as a grade 5

teacher. I throw the tap at him and stomp out. I stick my nose in the hall next door and a priest from Ottawa in an expensive suit is addressing a meeting of the Jungian Society and is telling them individuation is the work of a lifetime. On the subway a sensitive-looking man in a cowboy hat sits quietly looking straight ahead while a drunk with no hat at all looks at him and says you're not a cowboy, you're not smart enough. In the Costa Rica rainforest a bright red bird catches a butterfly in its beak and shakes off its shiny slightly iridescent blue wings before eating it. Practise love on animals, says Gurdjieff. They are more sensitive and respond better.

INVISIBLE ORCHARDS

This morning for breakfast I ate a cantaloupe
Grown where they spray with DDT.
It tasted a little like cleaning fluid.
You can't force a frightened tortoise
To re-extend its head and its limbs,
Not even if you strike it with an axe
(Ramakrishna). We search in vain
For flesh as sweet as is our brain.

My heart is full of apples and oranges
Each in a different state of decay.
My brain is full of slime-covered pins
Each pointing a different way.
God is the magnet, we are the pins
(Ramakrishna). Let's keep our pins clean.

The DDT goes down to the sea
After it passes through you and me.
Things my friends hate about themselves:
They don't like people who like Bob Dylan.
It takes them so long to learn simple things.
They talk about themselves too much.
Why can't they be like everyone else?

There's nothing to do but eat fruit and revel
    In our anonymity and emptiness.
        Simple problems demand complex solutions.
There's no need to be kind to yourself.

A tall menacing-looking woman
With a clipboard and a pen
Approaches four tiny Chinese
Women who zig and zag right by.

"Don't want that scribbler," one of them says.
This was last summer but I remember.
Alive in the cave of no return.
Stand back. I don't need any help.

Some have highly exaggerated notions
Of the impeccability of their taste in fruit.
What can be more impersonal than a body
Part, especially if it's your own?
When are we going to wake up
And appreciate the perfection of our dilemmas?
Our aim is to be conscious to the end.

Chinese subtitles: Cut the crab,
Time to explode the poison train.
It's blissful to bite into a fresh ripe plum.
It's obscene to give yourself top billing
In a world where people are forever killing
And soldiers in jeeps take food from the starving.

But a little misanthropy is mandatory.
You can't be ogling everyone on the street
Or falling in love with everyone you meet.
Temporary tattoos are the latest rage
Among those who make a virtue of their poor
Memories, our minds too full
Of baseball scores and movie ratings.
Did I break a tooth on the pit of that plum?

Or did I dream it? Life is sweet,
Pineapple-sweet, planting small trees
In the invisible orchards of our grief.

LAST FISHING WITH JACK

Jack wore his brown sports car cap
and me my gold-star cowboy hat
and we stopped the car in the graveyard
crumbling slowly down into the gorge
between Southampton and Chippawa Hill.

I carried my rod and the tackle box
and Jack his rod and the bait basket
and the path went almost straight down
maybe a hundred feet
into the last rapids of the Saugeen
before it widens and flows into Lake Huron
but we didn't know about Lake Huron
there in that strange gorge
rimmed with a crumbling graveyard
filled with the music of the rapids
music that goes on and on
down where the river divides into three
for a mile or so, leaving
two grassy treeless islands,
and we waded to the first
and then to the second.

There in pools among the rapids
we pulled out four small bass
and took them home for eating.
Down we went into the empire
of the last rapids of the Saugeen
for the last time forever, and brought it home.

NO MATTER

Carrying a sleeping child from the car to the house
in the wee small hours of the morning
a wee small crescent moon above the moving treetops

& the child softly waking up, & with a shock
saying "Oh Daddy look at that moon!
I like that kind of moon ..." & back to sleep

& no matter how long I live
how'll I be able to see a crescent moon
without hearing that voice,

pure voice of joy
& of moon.

FINGERS & TOES

Poems coming out of my hand —
out of my fingers & toes.
No matter how bad, my best
at this time & place, & true.
The music moving inside me,
coming out, covered with language.
Earth noises, murmurings of life
touching life, nature self-reflecting.

Who wants the poems?

If you want them take them, friend.
I be crazy to make them.
You be crazy to take them.
Take them in loaves as for lunch
& our fingers & toes will touch,
our bloodstreams one, as they are
surely in reality.
                    Touchings like this
seem good to me. Teaching ourselves
all we know, from the depths. And
maybe The Gods can be reminded
they made us in their own vision
& when we wake up in the next birth
we'll find ourselves blessed, & singing.

There's nothing for man but art & earth
and no hope but in seeing.

PICTURES IN PLAYBOY

Colour photography has really come a long way
since the Second World War —
I was looking at *Life*'s picture history
of the Second World War
particularly the colour plates
followed by the November 1967 *Playboy*
with shots of a $50,000 yacht
and all that warm pink flesh
bobbing around like rabbits in a hutch
climbing the masts, sunbathing on deck,
flying thru the air into the water.
Incitements to riot. In 1962
Playboy was great stuff but now
I can't separate it from Mao.

———————————

It's probably not the quality of the film
that has improved, but the photographers
know better how to handle it now, today.
But only a tiny fraction of the war's photos
were taken in colour, whereas
Viet Nam is different. Another thing
that is different is *Playboy*. And also
this poem. They are all entirely different.
Not connected in any way. Most poems
I write please me by their rebelliousness.
I never wrote a poem yet I kept
that didn't add a few lines to itself
when I wasn't noticing.

A FORM OF PASSION

This is the form my passion takes.

On a train heading into the night
he sat beside me and spoke as if
he'd known me all my life
yet he was less than half my age.
He was as black as this ink,
his face as perfectly shaped
as one of Shakespeare's better sonnets
radiant with intelligence
and a youthful arrogance
that was not at all obnoxious.

I can't remember what he said
but only that I was swamped with love
for this strange young African
                              and with a feeling
he understood me more deeply than anyone
had ever understood anyone before
or ever would again,
                    as if he had
tasted the marrow of my bones and
counted
        the hairs of my head.

I wanted to take him home.
I wanted to adopt him.

And suddenly I who had been suffering
from insomnia for years
fell asleep sitting up in the coach
as softly as a baby,
one moment intensely awake

and the next in the deepest sleep
and when I awoke it was dawn
and he was gone,
                    disembarked
at some night-stop on the prairie.

And later, at noon, the train
heading through the northern forest,
a tall blond man appeared
carrying a strange white hat in his hand,
a hat glowing with a life of its own
and delicately marked in an unknown script.
And when he saw me staring at his hat
he said: "Why are you staring like that?
You have one of your own just like it.
Why don't you ever wear it?"

He looked down at me with much sadness
as if he'd seen some glory in me that had long
been submerged in life's misery.

And when I told him I'd never seen a hat like that
and that I knew I certainly didn't own one
he insisted that I did.

And when I asked him where it was
he mumbled something about luggage
and then he disappeared.

Shaken, I knew I didn't have a hat like that
in my luggage or anywhere.
I'd never seen one like it.

THE INCHWORM

There was an inchworm on the curb, one end stuck to the curb and the
other end inching up into the air like a tiny rearing stallion. I stepped out
of the car and you said Look, there's an inchworm, and I said Oh yes,
look at it. When we're dead we won't be able to look at inchworms
but they'll be able to look at us, crawl all over us, inch by inch.
They are strange and I do not like them but I wouldn't want to kill one,
would much prefer to kill a mosquito any day. I had a friend once who
swallowed not an inchworm or a mosquito but a dragonfly. He was riding
his bicycle with his mouth open and a dragonfly flew down his throat. If
you've ever seen a dragonfly larva go through the intricate process of
splitting its skin to make way for the emergence of its adult form then
watched its adult form hanging from the leaf like a smudge of snot
then go darting away across the summer sky you'd agree that it was
a senseless way for anything so beautiful to meet its death. Some say
for every insect we kill deliberately that's another incarnation we have
to suffer, we have to be born and get murdered once for every bug we
step on. But inchworms aren't insects, they are worms, little living
units of measure, that's why I don't want to kill them, each inchworm
is a little word of God's language. I am glad there are no footworms.

Or yardworms. In the morning I woke and remembered seeing the
inchworm on the curb and thought it an image from a dream. I thought I'd
dreamt that we had seen an inchworm. As I was pouring coffee you phoned
and said Wasn't that a nice inchworm we saw yesterday? You mean
it wasn't a dream? I said. It was real, you said. Oh, I guess I woke up
thinking it was a dream, I said. It was like a dream, you said, it was
so clear the way the light was glistening on the curb and the worm and
there was something in the moment that made it all very dreamlike.

STILL LIFE WITH FRUIT

As the moon rises over the hill to the east
And the sun sets under the hill to the west
I'm alone in a log cabin on the Indian River
Watching the sky full of little pink clouds.
I'm eating a huge baked potato
And listening to the ball game on my short-wave radio.

Dozens of birds moonbathe on the lawn
And perch on the branches of nearby trees.
When I go out I bang the door
But they're slow to fly away
As if they know something's about to happen.
A mean-looking dog with something dead dangling
From its jaw turns and goes back to the river.

I haven't spoken a word in a week.
The best way to view an eclipse
Is to pretend you don't know it's about to happen.
You just happen to be admiring the moon
When that telltale bruise appears on one side.
The tip of a pine with a hawk's nest on a branch
Is silhouetted by the moon as it rises enveloped
By a pair of clouds translucent as an angel's
Wings in a skywide expanse of clarity.

Nothing on the horizon but low hills and high trees.
    And behind me the roof of my little cabin.
        Nothing is going to happen to the moon
            Except that its light is going to go out.
    If the moon's observant, it's been anticipating
This flash of obscurity since the previous one.

The thin transparent cloud catches
    The pale moonlight in its arms
        Reaching out like a crooner on the stage.
           It's three-two Toronto in the sixth
                At 2120 and through my binoculars
        A bruise the size of Australia and growing
    Has appeared on the famous face of the moon.
A shadow spreading faster than cancer.

A fifth of the moon's in darkness, the division
Between light and dark's jagged and irregular.
But through the binoculars it becomes a perfect
Hard-edged geometric arc.
The moon starts to resemble Brian Mulroney:
His jaw, his smile, the shape of his head,
Rising like a balloon of immense consequence.
And if my binoculars were slightly more powerful
I imagine I'd see pictograms on the surface.
I walk around the cabin and there's the Big Dipper.

The moon has two faces, one dark and one light,
    Like that Etruscan mug with the African girl
        On one side and the blonde on the other.
           The moon is a grenade about to explode
    In slow motion, the dark half
Has become a molten copper colour.

Three small aircraft in the last half hour
have flown across the face of the moon,
Atop the dark portion of which
A bright red light like a cherry sits:
A still life with fruit, a banana of light,
To the side of a fat pineapple with a cherry on top,
But a few minutes later it looks like an acorn.

The banana shrinks to a contact lens
Of light, and the moon is a giant eye
Waiting for long-lost constellations
To appear over the western hills.
And three meteors in five minutes
Laser across the moon's plump dullness.
Just me and the radio and the shooting stars.

And the moon smouldering. All the dull shades
Of red and orange and the bright banana fringe
Have bled together and the moon has become
A ripe Niagara peach hanging in the sky.
Lee Mazzilli hits a blooper to centre field
And two runs score in the eighth. Toronto's
Won fifteen straight in Fenway Park
And the moon has become a transparent fruit:
Red core, orange pulp and yellow skin.

I later discover Cathy and Clifford
Adrift in Stony Lake in their canoe.
And people from all the little islands
Are also out in their canoes.
And at the midpoint of the eclipse
Forty-nine beavers appear on the lake
And form seven circles of seven, all males,
Furiously whacking the surface with their tails.

A SENSE OF DANGER

Knocking around in the basement early Sunday morning
in a foggy hangover trying to remember my name

I bumped into the old birdcage
— the little door was down —
& I started looking for the bird
sensing he was in some danger

then my name came to me
& I remembered the bird
had been dead two years.

ANOTHER MOUTH

Only 6 days old, Jennifer —
she doesn't even know her name
but radiates a pure intelligence
that expresses a flash of gratitude
when her big sister of 3
drops a flower
into her crib.

An hour later she
spews 3 ounces of curdled milk
down her mother's dress.

———————

For all my life I felt so alone
and now suddenly I'm split in 4.

———————

I sit smoking a cigar —
Alison walking past my chair
stops for a moment, looking up
in frozen recognition —
like a Canadian tourist in the bronze shadow
of the Daibutsu Buddha of Kamakura.

My slightest movement is charged with importance —
the sparrows come in and out of my nostrils,
building nests in the hollow womb of my brain.

SLOW BLACK DOG

Meditating in the back
of Jack's green Volkswagen
rolling along Highway 2
east of Paris

I'm conscious only of the motion
of things speeding against me
on both sides of my head,
eyes closed, and a sudden braking

and a breaking of that dream.
I'm in a moving car among green hills
and cow grazings of the world,
motels, gas stations of Ontario

and a dog slowly walking across
into our speeding lane, a black dog,
and in tall grass at roadside, a boy,
waving his arms, screaming.

NEW YORK

Frank O'Hara used to say he couldn't enjoy a
blade of grass unless there was a subway handy;
he spent a month in Boston and when he returned
complained about how provincial they were up there.
This year five people already have been killed
by pieces of masonry falling from tall buildings
and eleven people have been killed by demonic comics
who sneak up behind people in subway stations
when the moon is full and push them in front of trains
but there is no fear in New York for I am here
walking with friends down Fifth Avenue on Easter Sunday.
There is a De Chirico exhibit at the Museum of Modern Art
but it is so warm and sunny outside and the streets are so full
of happy people gawking at the fire eaters and the trumpet trios
in front of St. Patrick's Cathedral, and here is a religious
argument, an old guy with bad teeth is holding a Bible
and yelling at this young ordinary-looking guy
and telling him to wipe that smile off his face
because the Bible is serious business
and the young guy says Christ put that smile on my face
and I'm not taking it off, and the old guy tells the young guy
he's a coward, too cowardly to get down on his knees and pray,
and the young guy is a little embarrassed, a crowd is forming,
and I yell out yeah, get down, get down, and the young guy
gets down on his knees with a sigh and he and the old guy pray
and Valerie and I walk on, we seem to have lost Sarah and Kenny
and Jim but we know they'll show up.

                              In an Indian restaurant
I overhear a man saying to a woman I know what you're going to say
and I agree with you, and I think that could have been me.
And I overhear a stockbroker ask his friend
is that Copper Lake any good? And as Frank O'Hara

lay on his death bed
in Bayview General Hospital
in Mastic Beach
dying of abdominal injuries
after being hit by the left fender of a dune buggy on Fire Island
he joked with the nurse who was French
and insisted on speaking French with her
and Valerie bought a canvas bag marked MoMA
at the Museum of Modern Art where O'Hara used to work
and now I am heading west into British Columbia
where everything is beautiful
and the air is pure
and the water is pure
and there is a general lack of urban blight
and in a moment I will board the plane for Vancouver
and there will be a small delicate sophisticated woman in her thirties
sitting next to me and reading French newspapers
and she will order Tia Marias and milk
and I will order Bloody Marys
and we will taste each other's breakfasts
and we will talk about Bonnard and Matisse
and I will tell her about Frank O'Hara
and she will tell me about Mayakovsky
how he was always striking up wonderful conversations
with strange and beautiful women in public places
and we will confess to each other
that we are primarily interested
in the quiet life.

THE PINK

In the vase are two dahlias,
one pink and one red. They were
both cut at the same time
but the pink one is as fresh as then
while the red one is limp
and getting limper.
                    From my view
the red one is partially behind the pink.
The pink is so new it is staggering.
Fresh as a fresh shirt under cellophane
but much more personal. It talks:
says hey there you are a lover
but I am love (note: the author at intense
peaks of pleasure will sometimes
get glimpses of a human flower-nature)
and all I can think of is its death,
being dead tomorrow or the next day
and of its being a regular offshoot
of that gnarled old root I must dig up
at the end of this month and dry out
for winter storage, and split up
in the spring for planting.

THE DAILY SCREAM

Monday morning I got up thinking ah Saturday morning
& made some Saturday-type phone calls
amazed to find out it was Monday

realizing what made me think of Saturday
was a long dark Saturday dream
that carried me through to the phone
                                        blank

& then perplexed I heard that vile laughter
in the air that vile mocking of human confusion
mocker of the sadness & diseases of those I love
laughing at the growing old & dying of my precious flesh
poking fun
                at the perfect beauties that are gone in a flash
                & the eternal slaughter,

some kind of elusive electric-vibration laughter
invisible but all around me
                        & so help me, friends

I vow not to rest till it slips
                        becomes visible

then god help it, goddammit.

HOLY DAYS IN A LAKE HURON RESORT TOWN

Folk burnt out need a vacation.
— The Confucian Odes (III-2-IX-4)

I

The cedars of Southampton are 40 feet high,
      grow in clumps,
      each trunk
      a perfect Japanese brush stroke —

a red Pontiac Grande Parisienne stops at the stop sign
then turns right
             past the red mailbox
             past the red fire hydrant,
             kicks up a little rainwater

& a boy in a red sweater walks out
from under the drooping branches of cedar
             — this at dusk

& hours later, full summer night
the corner lit by a single street lamp
from the red mailbox telephone pole
showing fully the red of the mailbox
& a few feet away the fire hydrant dull orange.

"What is the sense of sticking down here when you can do good …"
Silhouetted human beings walk by in clumps —
"Me, I break my mumumu …"
Voices spurt out & die onanistically
& a silhouette steps up to the mailbox,
posts a letter, & the light on his shoulders
shows a blue shirt.

First night in our Southampton summer home
& the cedars are a little glum
because there's no breeze for their branches.

Southampton where Lake Huron long ago agreed
to take in the Saugeen River
& the island called Chantry it wasn't expecting.
This afternoon we drove 125 miles northwest from Hamilton
through heavy rain all the way
                    my right leg aching
                    my matches wet —

We got to the lake & saw three gulls swooping
& a white sailboat sailing
& I remembered it was Sunday —
no beer.

The sexy little lighthouse on Chantry Island,
you must have seen it in pictures,
& a 12-year-old girl all by herself in the rain
under a floppy orange hat.

    II

The sun shines!
Shadows run among the cedars.

With our log cabin come three green lawn chairs
& a red picnic table
all spotted with fresh gullshit.
For two hours I sit at the picnic table
drinking beer, watching the gullshit dry —

when the gullshit is sufficiently dry
I brush it away.

My wife & kids play in the sandbox.

The sun fades & thunder comes up on the lake.
Soon it's raining.

III

The Southampton train only comes once a day
so it goes overboard on its whistle.

As for the Saugeen Lighthouse it lets go a three-second blast
three times a minute.
                    17 seconds of tense silence.
                    3 seconds of profound ecstasy.
                    The gulls ignore it.

Tonight I stand on the north pier
wondering where the river would be said to end
& the lake begin
& three ghostly gulls followed by a fourth
come whistling out from behind a secret grove of water willows
flying out in a row across the mouth of the river
18 inches above the water
disappearing into nothingness on a path pointing
at Chantry Island
                    home of snakes & shipwrecks.

After sundown the sky began to clear in patches.
Now the top of a full moon tips the eastern cedars.
Now, that terrifying inevitability.

A 1956 Chev roars through the stop sign,
loses control momentarily, trims the lawn,
knocks over a neatly stacked pile of garbage bags,
regains control & quickly is out of earshot down the road.
The streetlights didn't even blink!

Two boys follow two girls down the unlit street.
"Hello … Hi … What's your names? … Where you going?"
No answers from the girls. Boys drop back a bit, giving up.
"Sure you don't know what time it is?" (another weak try)
I yell out through the dark screened porch:
"It's 10:45."

IV

This morning the raindrops are fighting like dogs & cats,
cedar bark black with damp

> pane
>
> rain
>
> pain

Silver streams running down the screens full of light.
It's raining all over Ontario,
a cold rain falling through warm unmoving air.
On the beach the sand is soaked as far down as I can scoop
& there are no gulls.

V

Hot sun at slow work of evaporating Lake Huron,
putting a little dry dust back into Bruce County,
blondes turning pink then red along all the wide beaches
    of the long Bluewater Highway (21).

On the beach at Southampton my four-year-old daughter
chews bread for the gulls.

No gulls come, little girl in yellow so sad
throwing crumbs with compassion ignored
crumbles up the last piece of bread & tosses it.
A lone gull floats overhead 20 feet high,
doubles back at 19 feet, you can see interest there,
but silent as a ghost, holding his breath, thinking —

Soon 60 gulls are swarming sparring screaming scrambling
each perfect warm-blooded warp of the wind
sawing at the crumbling sand with delicate bill-blades,
little girl towering over the action wondering what was the delay

& sunbathers cock their ears at all the screeching noise —
"Hey, look at all the seagulls over there!"
"The little girl's feeding them."
"Oh, I thought maybe somebody died."

    VI

The four of us drive the 21 miles into Owen Sound
& halfway there the odometer flicks over to 69000
& as usual I look at all the passing licence plates
looking for a licence number that'll match my mileage
69001 69002 69003, all the time looking
with no luck, not even close.

                              & I've got a whistle
plastic, imitation of a little tree with a bird on it —
& if you finger the end it sounds like a gull
& everyone we pass we give him the whistle
& he turns into a big fat toad.

A car speeding down the highway at 60
& we give it the whistle & suddenly it's empty
except for four frantic toads hopping around on the seats —

A girl in a bikini, sitting on a picnic bench —
I slow down real slow & give her a good whistle
& she loves it, doesn't turn into a toad, smiles, blows me a kiss —
& I turn & laugh at my wife's mock anger.

We pass the little village of Springmount.
Joan wants to know how it got that name.
I remind her of the Niagara Escarpment,
that this is the same Mountain we know down Hamilton way
& what Niagara Falls falls over & she doesn't believe me
until the road starts to go down down slowly into Owen Sound
& she notes that it does look a lot like the Mountain
as she knows it around Ancaster-Stoney Creek way.

We get to the new Towers department store in Owen Sound
& in the huge parking lot are 69,000 parking spaces
all occupied.
                    Turns out it's Fred Flintstone Day
& there's been a big turnout for free balloons & colouring books
& hourly appearances of Fred & Barney & local personalities
& what guy wouldn't take his kids to see the Flintstones, free?
We get back in the car & drive downtown.
The old shopping areas are the best & most deserving of our dough.
There's a lot of interesting things in downtown Owen Sound.
A bearded artist (they're the best) is painting a sign two storeys
above the main corner,
two shirtless guys are laying a sewer & chatting
with passersby.

Tom Thomson's ghost returns hourly to the Tom Thomson Museum &
      Art Gallery,
& someone else real famous was born in Owen Sound —
I thought it was Nelson Ball, Joan thought it was Robert Goulet,
turned out we were both wrong it was David W. Harris.

An old guy is trying to peek through a crack in a board fence
to see a construction site, but the crack's too narrow.
I pass by and he says,
"Sure putting 'em up fast these days, ain't they?"

Having lost my green pen I'll continue this poem in blue ink.

VII

Another day is done. The red sun, swollen to twice its normal size
is setting over blue broad Lake Huron. At the foot of Southampton's High
    Street
a crowd of tourists, cars neatly parked, have gathered to watch the spectacle.
The early birds sit on benches, latecomers stand tall & peaceful —
all staring quietly at the slowly setting silent sun.
The lake is blue & full of other wondrous colours, the sun at this stage
turns the sky inside out & all souls have depths of pink & orange forever.

In Babylon he who glanced at the setting sun would die that night.
It's hard today to pick up on that way of thinking. There was a secret society,
the members had tried to commit suicides by sunset glances
& now had inexpressible secrets. They naturally aided the Greeks.

High Street of Southampton & Lake Huron sunset No. 5,475,000 —
the sun is about halfway into the sea, a critical point, will it change its mind?
No way, & suddenly all the tourists, mostly elderly, women in long dresses,
flowers in their wigs, old men in suits & ties, eyes fading but on the make,
they all turn away from the lake, walking back to cars & nearby tourist homes.
I alone am left to watch the sun's last spark of the day unalterably extinguished
with an inaudible softly resigned moan here on the Ontario side of Lake
    Huron,
northeastern quarter of North America, Labrador icy against the back of my
    neck.
They left me here alone, is it a trick, to see the last drop of the sun,
& is something strange going to happen to me tonight, have I been a fool?

VIII

An hour later the sky is dark
but there is light among the western clouds,
clouds newly arrived from beyond the blue horizon,
& long red patches of tremendous shape,
Chantry Island a silhouette,
Chantry Lighthouse blink blink blink.

I sit on an overturned rowboat
near water's edge
                    & the little waves coming in
bring a peace to my saddened soul,
ripples breaking into surf in my head.

A light speeds across the horizon
pinpoint of light
                   moving at least 4 miles in 20 seconds.
Probably the water-level reflection of a high-flying plane,
flying high enough to catch the sun's rays & bounce them
forward an hour into the night.

Four girls, about 17, walk by pulling faces at me.
I watch them out of the corner of my eye
then suddenly I make a quick bear-like growl
& they run away.

                  Saddened soul of sunsets.
Night now dark, no moon till much later,
but far above me the Big Bear stars,
& on the western horizon fresh clouds of lightning.
The waves are higher, coming up higher on the beach.
I kick off my moccasins & let my toes drink.

28 years old & a million problems,
no room here for a saddened soul.

My psychopathic death-worshipping days are done.

So busy giving my wife & kids something to chew on.

Somehow I keep returning to lightning on the horizon,
fantastic cedar vistas, insane gulls, my lungs.

IX

Tossing horseshoes with my wife.
She says she's trying but she doesn't aim!

Clumps of cedar surround the pitch.
"One thing, you kill more ants than I do."

The cedars are hissing with the wind.
Horseshoes thud & clang.

X

Tobermory is pronounced Tubbermurray by the residents,
that's why you often hear it referred to as The Tub.
— Greg Curnoe

Strolling along the beach at 5 a.m.,
crescent moon pointing towards the unrisen sun,
the stars giving off light of their own, light of their own.

The stars are as far away from each other as they are from us.
That's hard to believe, says my wife.

For the Apollo 11 to bump into a star is about the same chance
as for me to reach for a beer & bump into Tobermory.
Do I really believe that?

On the beach at midnight I met two very nice Southampton residents,
Danny Whitehead who gets busted for underage beer & smashing cars
& Carol Bates who is going to be a nurse.

XI

On the pier at the mouth of the Saugeen, 5 a.m.,
talking to an old angler. "Hi Ed, remember me?"

He's got soft-shelled crabs, threads one on his hook,
lets it drop into 6 feet of water lapping the pier.

These are the same crabs whose white-bleached shells you see
among the rocks at water's edge at Baie du Doré or Miramichi Bay.

Locally Baie du Doré is pronounced Bet Door.

"Wreckt my car last September," says Ed, gets a bite, sets his hook.
Pulls in nothing. Fish so big it took his hook, snapt his line.

"That was a sheephead, he'll have a sore mouth for a couple weeks."

"Hit some gravel, complete wreck, only 21 miles on it — 21,000.
Had to get a new one. Was in hospital at Fergus for a month.
Had a mild 'cussion, broke my clerical bone & cut my leg.
You lose a lot when you wreck a car, all those extras, front & rear
    speakers.
Soon's I got out I got a new car & drove to Florida for two months.
Can't stand the winters now with my clerical bone."

Spent a half hour with him & he caught two bass, both keepers.

The whole sky clouded over from the northeast just before dawn.
An hour later the sky cleared & it was another day.

XII

I took the kids to the Laundromat, the Brewers Retail, the Snack Wagon for a cone,
then out to the Dam Project 3 miles upstream at the rapids.
Indians who'd worshipped these rapids for thousands of years
would have been amazed, even as I was amazed.

XIII

First time I've swum in waves this big since a kid in Lake Erie
but even then Lake Erie was more full of crap than Huron is today
& I try to make it out to the Big Flat Rock & make it
but can't hang on, get smashed into the small rocks.

Probably even wavier over in front of the Bowling Alley
so I go over there — this is where I always swam two years ago —
& man, there's no beach left, waves smashing
against the grassy dunes, the dunes crumbling,
the grass turns black & snaky in the foam.

Four old guys making a movie on the beach, clouds & storm —
trees bending over in loops, gulls flying backwards —
I jump up & down hamming it up for the film,
then get picked up & tossed by a perfect breaker.

I remember Bill Davies swimming outside the pier at Port Elgin
in the middle of a huge storm with lightning.
"It's great to see the lightning skip along the surface,
sizzling, & be right there swimming through it all."

(Coincidental with my writing of this last, I was later to find out,
old Bill Davies was suffering an almost-fatal heart attack.)

Suddenly two young women fully clothed run screaming into the surf.
I didn't see where they came from, transparent joy.
The four old guys drop their camera & stare stupidly,
blow good footage by lack of cool.

"This poem isn't finished yet!"
— Victor Coleman

"Be sure to put a proper ending on it."
— Joan A. McFadden

MICKEY MOUSE

When I was a kid I looked through a keyhole and thought I saw
Mickey Mouse. After that, whenever I was in the vicinity of that
particular keyhole I would look through, hoping to see Mickey Mouse
again. But he never reappeared. It took several months before I gave
up, sad because the natural visionary ability of childhood was
beginning to fade.

On Monday I told you I would be staring at you from a distance
on Tuesday. On Tuesday I looked through the window of the bank
and saw you talking to the manager. You looked over your shoulder at
me. On Wednesday you wrote a poem in which this incident was
mentioned. On Thursday you mailed me the poem. On Friday I
received it. On Saturday I walked past the bank and looked through
the window but no one was there.

On Saturday when I got home my house was full of fresh fruit
and camera equipment. The note said you had gone looking for
Easter eggs in the tall grass (this was October) and you had found all
these zucchinis, squashes, vegetable marrows, apples, pears, plums,
tripods, zoom lenses, light meters.

It's midnight. I'm alone. In the distance a dog is barking. I am
wondering about that vision of Mickey Mouse. My head is sweet with
the taste of the plums.

THE BIG M

1. Every Sunday at noon during the summer the guy next door (Frank by name) treats his kids to a big watermelon. They mill about on the verandah and lawn eating big slices of it, and it is funny to hear, as the well-dressed devout file out of Garside Gospel Church ("Where the HOLY BIBLE is WHOLLY TAUGHT") half a block away, bells chiming, neat fussy Frank in a booming voice call out, "Be careful what you do with the seeds."

2. I'm in my cellar study
keeping cool

writing this poem quickly
because Joan is coming DOWN
with a KNIFE

and a cold
watermelon.

3. bpNichol hates watermelon.

NOTES

Cover photo: Taken in spring 1968 by Mac Rymal, a friend of the author's, in front of Mac's house on Glennie Avenue in the far east end of Hamilton, Ontario. Mac was a journalist in Hamilton before he moved to Ottawa to further his career, then to Vancouver to a teaching position at Langara College. He committed suicide at fifty-seven. The Mac Rymal Memorial Scholarship is awarded each summer. Directly across the street is the house where Bill Mykes grew up. Bill, a dear friend of the author from age twelve, was editor of the *Stoney Creek News* for several years, studied at McMaster University and later taught in the faculty of science at the University of Alberta, learned to fly, then took a very interesting job with B.C. Power. In his late forties he died of cancer in his West Vancouver home. The sad little girl is Alison Janet McFadden, who had been having a little difference of opinion with her friend Janet Rymal. Alison eventually grew up to be a very strong woman, but after a long and agonizing illness she passed away, on January 16, 2000, at the McMaster University Medical Centre. When editor Stuart Ross was presented with these details, he rightly declared that the photo was "pregnant with tragedy." The young man trying to wipe away Alison's tears is the author of this book.

Desire Blossoms: The final poem in *Five Star Planet*. Editor Stuart Ross was at first keen on using *Desire Blossoms* as the title for this *Selected*. But *Why Are You So Sad?* won out at the end. "Desire Blossoms" is full of interesting but unpleasant memories and images, and it seems fitting that it should be the first poem in the book, if it couldn't be the title poem.

Travellin' Man: An early poem based on an ordinary domestic situation and a memory or two.

American Squirrel: Karl Siegler of Talonbooks was the editor of *Five Star Planet*, in which this poem first appeared. After reading an earlier version of the poem, he suggested that it takes more than tossing a seed on the ground to make an apple tree grow. At his suggestion, the penultimate stanza was added. This might be the first (and last) poem to rhyme "carcasses" with "parkas as."

Nature: The notion of nature never committing an error must have had a liberating impact on the author's mind way back when. As for the two branches of the tree falling to the ground on the night before they were to be pruned, it's not that amazing a coincidence really; it's too long ago to determine with any certainty, but perhaps the author intended to prune the branches simply because they looked as if a good wind might knock them down and it did before he had a chance to. Also, it is true that on the day Alison was born, the author accidentally fell and broke his toe, as the *I Ching*, which had been consulted the previous night, had predicted.

Three on a Tree: The idea of the coach biting the heads off live sparrows to inspire his players was taken from a newspaper article.

Number: The author insists on the factuality of this poem, though he claims never to have eaten seven ice cream cones in a row. And his mother had only two children.

My Brother's Poetry: The imagination continues to bounce up and down on the trampoline of factuality.

Eckankar: Written in 1979 or 1980 during the author's three-year event-filled residence in beautiful Nelson, B.C.

Little Spots of Grease: Today one might say that this woman appeared to be a full-blown Taoist, or a natural-born Pantheist. Her mind and heart seemed perennially empty, and she had less self-consciousness than a two-year-old. Her individuality was submerged in the universe. She was in a state of nirvana. And this quality was with her all her years, whenever she showed up. She had an ego-less invisibility, was always alone, and no one ever even glanced at her. The late Paul Kidd was a well-known newspaper reporter with a reputation for tough-minded eccentricity; he was quick to anger and not easy to get along with. His explanations for his top-secret plan to smuggle razor blades into Yugoslavia never made sense. Even he seemed unable to notice this woman.

Eight Inches of Snow: A poem which at first exhibits a lot of anxiety then dwindles to a state of extreme tranquillity. The turtle was named after the Russian ballerina Natalia Romanovna Makarova, who was born the same year as the author and defected to the United States in 1970. She returned to Russia in 1990, retiring after one performance with the Kirov Ballet.

On the Road Again: An attempt to describe a momentary experience of unconditional love of country. Sir Walter Scott does it more memorably in his "Lay of the Last Minstrel." At a press conference a few years ago, journalist Helen Thomas told President George W. Bush that "to understand the Iraqi resistance, I suggest reading the Scottish poet Sir Walter Scott. He wrote: 'Breathes there a man with soul so dead who never to himself has said this is mine own my native land.'"

Country Hotel in the Niagara Peninsula: A split-level poem, with what appears at first to be no apparent connection between the two stanzas.

Death of a Man Who Owned a Swimming Pool: A fictional poem, tragic but totally made up, a little on the political side, with the author imagining himself as Snoopy, the clever pup in *Peanuts*.

The Spill: It's as if the author is describing a wide-angle snapshot to a blind friend.

When I Am Dead: Thomas Hardy had the knack of sentimentalizing himself without being offensive about it. Few can do that. And even he didn't try it very often. This poem represents my first attempt at rhyme since high school. For a more condensed version, see my poem "After Thomas Hardy's 'Afterwards.'"(on p. 181).

Beverly Report: Sometimes a little poem, like a photo, will give added life to a fast-fading memory.

Margaret Hollingsworth's Typewriter: This is a good one about poetic hyperbole, urgency, embarrassment, stubbornness, self-torture, forgiveness and high drama. At no extra cost, it features one of Canada's most brilliant playwrights.

Baseball Loneliness: Just another poem featuring dreams about baseball, the cinema and childhood memories.

Lennox Island: The author is proud to have received an unsolicited compliment on this poem from none other than the legendary Prince Edward Island poet Milton Acorn.

The Slippery Wig: The hard-luck side of a fading Steeltown.

This Poem Has a Good Title: Can poems save the world? Read this and decide for yourself.

My Criminal Record: Giving a futuristic spin to the idea of crime and punishment.

Poem for Jennifer to Read Many Years from Now: Jenny recently told me she still remembers trying to pick my words off the page as I sat writing.

The Rockies: A meditation on the ease and painlessness with which we kill large numbers of innocent people from great distances.

A Moment in the Life of the Members of the Graduating Class of Arnprior High School, 1976: The Ottawa Valley is very beautiful during spring thaw.

Lion in the Road: The Toronto mindset seems to be improving since this poem was written. It's no longer all that cool to be too cool for words. If you see somebody on Yonge Street who is very cool, he's probably from Hamilton.

For Dwight Eisenhower on His Death: This poem gives me pleasure because it dares to say that all deaths are equal, the deaths of the imperialists and the deaths of the indigenous. Unfortunately, I was wrong to say that "Gasoline Alley" had been cancelled by the *Globe and Mail*. Turns out it just didn't appear for a day or two.

The Death of Greg Curnoe: This poem appeared in my book *There'll Be Another* with this note: "During two days and two nights of convalescence in my fourth Havana hotel, from a touch of food poisoning contracted in my third, I wrote this poem.... Back in Canada, Sheila Curnoe and Christopher Dewdney, both of whom had accompanied Greg on his trip to Cuba a few years earlier, kindly shared their memories and read the manuscript. I hereby call upon the Canadian Minister of External Affairs to begin petitioning the Cuban government for the return of Greg's notebooks." George Bowering's *The Moustache: Memories of Greg Curnoe* (Coach House Press, 1993) is a true account of this bright and beautiful painter, whose works remain on display in the London art gallery, the Art Gallery of Ontario, the National Gallery in Ottawa and elsewhere. It's hard to imagine how Curnoe would be able to thrive in today's atmosphere of artistic gloom and political hopelessness; I sometimes find myself feeling almost glad that he died when he did.

Dying Metaphors: It was the poet Lionel Kearns who first tipped me off about this list of World War II clichés compiled by George Orwell in his now famous and oft-published 1946 essay, "Politics and the English Language." Mandatory reading.

Love's Golden Splendor: Another short poem of two stanzas, with each stanza illuminating the other.

1940: A strange poem about poetry, perhaps overly personal in places and easy to dislike, but I like it.

The Searchlight: Insomniac Press editor Paul Vermeersch very nicely made a special request for the inclusion of this poem, even though it hadn't appeared in an actual book. It was published as a postcard by Véhicule Press in Montreal, then almost got lost.

Kitsilano Beach on a May Evening: There was electricity in the air, and with every step a fresh memory popped into my mind.

Strange Language: At sixty-four, Mother had a serious fall from which she never fully recovered.

Frank O'Hara: This piece might contain a certain amount of poetic embroidery, which is understandable since the trip to New York took place way way back in the spring of 1954. My imagination insists every word is true, but who can believe every word his imagination says is true?

Parenthood: Pretty well everyone I know remembers how old they were when they first read *For Whom the Bell Tolls*.

Child Molesters: A better poem than the title would indicate. I'd change the title, but at this stage that would seem wrong.

Early Autumn Guitar: Nobody knows whom this poem is about. Not even the person this poem is about. Not even me.

My Body Was Eaten by Dogs: I often tried to figure out where this poem came from. I knew I'd never been to Oxyrhynchus. And then, just now, after all those years, I remembered: it came from a dream.

The Portable Nietzsche: It was my friend Al J. Plant who first told me about Bill Davies, and coincidentally Al also told me the story recounted in "Darryl & the Moose." Bill died in 1969 and "The Portable Nietzsche" was written soon after that. In re-reading it now after close to forty years, I'm amazed at how sane and relatively ordinary I made Bill seem. The fact is, Bill, though capable of great feats of sanity, and possessed of a great gift for kindness and friendship, did have a very crazy side. He not only showed his crazy side on numerous occasions, he often told me crazy things he had done long before I met him. But for some odd reason I chose not to dwell on that in the poem. I'll just keep it to myself. I will say that his level of skill as a practitioner of yoga was astonishing. It was a simple matter for him to suddenly jump onto the counter of his bookstore, stand on his head and, with great ease, perform the very difficult *urdwapadmasana,* with his full-grown pet boa constrictor, Gabriella, wrapped around his waist, and sometimes with a lit cigarette in his mouth and blowing smoke rings. Also he enjoyed performing the peacock posture on his pinball machine, and when new customers came in he often would greet them by prancing around the floor on his hands while doing the *kukutasana.* He insisted he never had yoga lessons (there were none to be had in those days); rather, he picked it all up, when he was in his early teens, from a "Speaking of Pictures" photo spread in the February 24, 1941 issue of *Life,* simply by emulating the photos. Bill would facetiously call himself Jagananda, because he was so fond of his sports car. He became a close friend of Swami Vishnudevananda, though they seemed to have had a falling out just before Bill's death. Bill claimed that his only guru was Swami Yogananda, who had died in 1952, and said that he often took teachings from Yogananda while the two were in the astral plane. Although of Welsh origins, Bill towards the end of his life began to resemble Yogananda. I have the photos to prove it.

Standing Invitation: Just another Northern Ontario fantasy.

The Cooling Spell: Just another Hamilton city morgue fantasy.

A Father Flirts with His Daughter: Definitely not a fantasy. The three twos, then a few days later another three twos inside a five, it all actually happened exactly as described. When you keep your eyes open, and are willing to be generous, money will come your way.

Crazy Bus: One long skinny Hamilton dream. It's very hard to avoid looking at a plane in a dream, especially if you know that as soon as you do look at it, it will explode in a ball of flame.

Sad Old Notebooks: The thrill of making love on a train and learning to play backgammon on a bus.

The Golden Treasury of Knowledge: Tips on the best way to wake up in the morning. And when will that final alarm clock ring?

Stormy January: A medicine for homesickness.

The Armadillo: This was probably inspired by an incident in grade 10. Somebody after hours carved my name on my desk. The furious teacher refused to believe I was innocent, until I asked if he really thought I was stupid enough to do such a thing. Then he apologized.

Unchained Melody: Everything here is true, except it wasn't Mr. Baff who had the pigeons, it was another man who lived on the next street and I never knew his name.

A Cup of Tea with Issa: Another Nelson, B.C., poem, with references to Hamilton and Japan.

The Seduction of Queen Elizabeth II: It's true, I did nip over to Buckingham Palace, but I did not seduce the Queen.

Tibetan Monologue: A mantra to calm the stormiest seas.

Secrets of the Universe: Another Nelson, B.C., poem. The woman spoke with such confidence, and had me almost convinced that she had danced with me on other planets. Apparently this is the poem that initially inspired editor (and poet) Stuart Ross to wish to edit this book.

Meaningless Midnight Musings: Some of the elements of this poem are not all that meaningless. For instance, it was very startling when the neighbours became so excited about Allen Ginsberg arriving on the scene. Hard to imagine a poet today whose presence would create such a stir in Hamilton, or anywhere.

Dead Hippopotamus: This was the final poem of the one hundred in *Gypsy Guitar*. It was intended to be a grand resolution, but in retrospect it just added to the absurdity. That whole "cowboy in Alberta" episode happened so long ago, it was before I started publishing poems, but I can still see that bewildered calf and the stinking carcass of its mother. In those days I thought I'd be eighteen forever. Then something went wrong.

An Unexpected Cheque for $86: When the news came that Jack Kerouac was dead, I consoled myself by realizing that he'd always be there for me in his books. But dammit, I'd never get to meet him!

Thin Gypsy Woman: An anorexic Gypsy sleeps over. As she sleeps the poet writes, revealing rather unpleasant aspects of his character. After "Una Strana Zingarella" by Dino Campana (1885-1932).

Pop: The same Alison who is on the front cover of this book — and the same Pop!

An Inventory of My Possessions: I still have John B. Boyle's "Spanish Heel," my father's dog tags, the grey double-breasted suit and a surprising number of other things.

An Hour's Restless Sleep: Can't think of any notes to make about this poem. It's definitely not Shakespeare. I had no problems with a friend who said it was the worst poem he'd ever read. But still...

After Thomas Hardy's "Afterwards": See "When I Am Dead" for a version of Hardy's poem that is closer to the original.

A Jar of Butterflies: Did I really write that? How strange! Not as strange though as a story by Edwidge Danticat, in which a mother instructs her thirteen-year-old daughter to crush living butterflies on her breasts to make them grow.

The Eskimo Who Lacked Perfection: The proper term was *Eskimo* then, but *Inuit* now. What to do? It seemed more authentic to leave it as it was.

Beer and Pizza: Hiroshima Day, the torching of the Toronto Women's Bookstore and two events involving spiders.

Pictograms by Starlight: Rilke may have long ago pronounced the death of bourgeois travel, but New Zealand is still a heavenly place to visit.

The Spoiled Brat: This poem is based on evidence given in a Hamilton courtroom. It's written in the first person, in the spirit of the interconnectedness of all humanity.

A Very Calm Demeanour: Somewhat reminiscent of a *cri de coeur* from Saul Bellow in *Humboldt's Gift*: "With everyone sold on the good how does all the evil get done?"

What Does It Mean ... : Tough questions, a few tentative answers and the Seven Ages of the Fruit Fly.

Walter's Moustache: It wasn't Walter's moustache that my grandmother was innocently fondling; it was the painter Greg Curnoe's moustache. And it wasn't my grandmother's first husband (from Cardiff) who was the pacifist who nevertheless went to war and was killed in his first battle; it was her second husband's older brother (from Sheffield). I have no recollection whatsoever of why I made these peculiar and senseless changes. Everything else in the poem is factually accurate. As in many of the poems in this book, everyone mentioned in this one is dead — except for me, and I'm fading fast.

Spirits Bay: Mistakenly referred to as "Spirit Bay" in its first publication. The more traditional name is Kapowairua. A remote spot, sacred to the Maori culture and far from any non-Maori settlements.

The Angel: A somewhat amiable piece, blending old memories, fresh dreams, current concerns and expressions of friendship.

Jane and Jean: This poem seemed to be very contrived, and so I didn't like it for a long time. But then, with a little help from my editor Stuart Ross and other friends, including the real-life Jean and the real-life Jane, I learned to like it fine.

Thirty-four Lines about Horses: I've just now noticed there's an unpleasant smugness about this poem. As if the author knows all kinds of things about horses that lesser beings don't know. I know nothing about horses, but I like them.

Flying over Indiana: There he goes, thinking he's Jesus again.

The Sky and I: Inspired by a series of dreams about rotting old caskets coming out of the earth, floating into the moonlit sky, and making clicking noises, and long moans and sighs.

Over at the Undermount: In Hamilton, on the east side of James Street North, a few steps up from the Toronto, Hamilton and Buffalo railway bridge. The Undermount is a pleasant pub, with a summer patio — and it's yet to be discovered by the tourists.

It's Unbelievable: I'm very happy with the poems Stuart Ross has selected for this book. Some of his selections I wouldn't have had the courage to make myself, such as "It's Unbelievable," for instance. Some selections seem quite odd, and some a bit embarrassing. But I'm convinced it's all in all a much better selection than anything I could have come up with. I'm proud to have stayed aloof from the selection process, though I did make two suggestions, I believe. And both were warmly accepted.

My Own True Nature: A grocery list of dreamlike events, mostly involving animals, and bracketed top and bottom by a few items of factual information.

A Sentimental Introduction: I don't seem to remember this pleasant mood lasting very long. Maybe more effort was required. Our lives are full of squandered moments of grace and lost opportunities.

The Iguana Within: Thought of writing a series of a hundred such attempts at turning public-relations handouts into poems. Soon realized one was enough.

After Reading Shiki's Poem about the Dead Dog Floating down the River: I first wanted to use "Dead Dog Floating down the River" as the title for this book, but ... cooler heads prevailed.

Letter to My Father: I think I forgot to send him this. Or did I type it out for him and tell him it was a recently discovered poem by Robert Frost? Can't remember now.

Darryl & the Moose: It's hard to believe that these two poetic sketches occurred in the far east end of Hamilton (probably Parkdale Avenue) on a hot summer afternoon in 1966, with no traffic, no pedestrians, complete silence. It seems more like the early fifties.

Four Experiments: From my more mature perspective today, I'd be tempted to call all four failed. The dark wasn't as dark as I thought it was.

Peace: That comment about Victor Coleman bears the trace of a long forgotten in-joke. Victor would be the last one I'd worry about, if I were a worrier.

Monkey on My Back: This is one of several "After Baudelaire" poems from *Gypsy Guitar*. They were based on readings of Baudelaire's "Little Prose Poems." As part of the challenge I had to read the poems in French, no translations allowed. I knew my French wasn't up to it, but I didn't want to be contaminated by even Baudelaire's most inspired translators. All I had was my desire. And my 1978 *Collins Robert*. And my knowledge that any similarity between Baudelaire and McFadden would be a lucky shot.

My Words/Hamilton: Aged ignorance refuses to consider the poems of youth. Perhaps for very good reasons.

It Would Be Nice to Go to Heaven with You: How smug and juvenile of me to have made fun of the name of one of the greatest blues singers. As for Ronn Metcalfe, his Big Band was based in St. Catharines and was well known through the fifties and sixties. He was a crusader, fighting to bring Big Band music back in business, when even his old friends Count Basie and Woody Herman knew it was finished. Metcalfe's final gig, possibly apocryphal, was leading the backup band for Chubby Checker.

Elephants: Unforgettable how the male so precisely took exactly one half of the portion of nuts being offered, while looking into my eyes to make sure I was noticing, then moved back and let the lady elephant move forward and take her portion. The male's eyes told me that although he was spending his life in leg chains he was still hanging on to his humanity. Unlike other animals he could name.

Moonkat: Poems blossom in foreign environments.

Last Chance to Hit Balls (Six Tanka and Six Haiku): *Tin Cup* is a 1996 golfing movie starring Kevin Costner.

Titles I Have Heard of but Not Read: The poem's theme was later picked up and recycled in the "Time Warp" chapter of *Great Lakes Suite* (Talonbooks, 1997).

Greaseball: This is of course a dream poem, as so many seem to be in this volume.

Sex with a Sixteen Year Old: Maybe I should have replaced "Sex" with "Flirtation," but it's too late now. One wouldn't change a word in a poem after the poem had been published, just as a painter wouldn't be allowed to mess with a work he had signed and sold.

Perceptual Error: My favourite bit is the cowboy on the subway. As for the cinema manager, that was fifteen years ago. People generally seem to be more able to control their anger lately. In spite of everything, we seem to be maturing, as Vladimir Putin has suggested.

Invisible Orchards: Life is sweet or did I dream it?

Last Fishing with Jack: First poem I wrote after burning all the poems I'd ever written.

Fingers & Toes: Second.

The Inchworm: Seems to be a bit too much hot air in stanza one. All talk, no action.

Still Life with Fruit: It was a stroke of luck to be alone in a log cabin on a clear calm night during such a brilliant lunar eclipse.

Holy Days in a Lake Huron Resort Village: Victor Coleman found the title pretentious, but I somehow knew it had to be. I understand the cedars have all been cut down and the log cabins have been removed to make room for a hotel.

The Big M: Three watermelons on a Sunday afternoon, and a surprise appearance from the late great bpNichol.

INDEX OF POEMS

Note: The parenthesized abbreviation beside each index entry refers to the book the poem originally appeared in. A key to these abbreviations appears directly below.